Cello

To our favourite cellist
on her thirteenth
birthday.

Many Happy Returns
Lesley-Ann

from Mum &

YEHUDI MENUHIN MUSIC GUIDES

Available
Violin and Viola by Yehudi Menuhin and William Primrose
Piano by Louis Kentner
Clarinet by Jack Brymer
Oboe by Leon Goossens and Edwin Roxburgh
Percussion by James Holland
Musicology by Denis Stevens

In preparation
contributions on
Bassoon by William Waterhouse
Flute by James Galway
Harpsichord and early keyboard instruments by Igor Kipnis
Horn by Barry Tuckwell
Organ by Arthur Wills
Voice edited by Sir Keith Falkner

YEHUDI MENUHIN MUSIC GUIDES

Cello

William Pleeth

Compiled and edited by
Nona Pyron

MACDONALD & CO
LONDON & SYDNEY

First published in Great Britain in 1982 by
Macdonald & Co (Publishers) Ltd
London & Sydney

Maxwell House
74 Worship Street, London EC2A 2EN

ISBN Cased: 0 356 07864 7
    Limp: 0 356 07865 5

Filmset, printed and bound in Great Britain by
Hazell Watson & Viney Ltd, Aylesbury, Bucks

Contents

List of Illustrations

YEHUDI MENUHIN MUSIC GUIDES

Introduction
by Yehudi Menuhin

If any instrument has a deep and visceral appeal it is the cello. It reaches our emotions on a deep and profound level and it seems to me that what a teacher of the instrument must among many other things struggle to convey is the reach, the power and the amplitude of the cello. Long years of happy association have served to confirm my admiration for a man with just this ability – my beloved and trusted colleague Bill Pleeth.

There is I suppose the question of vision; it is his imparting of this that has made some of the most unsurpassed advocates of the cello. Curiously enough, when I awarded Jacqueline du Pré, then still in her teens, her first prize at the Royal College of Music some twenty years ago, I exclaimed as soon as I heard her: 'She must be a student of Bill Pleeth.' Of course that was the case. And Jacqueline adds her own touching tribute to her old teacher in this book.

The reader can imagine, therefore, my pleasure in introducing William Pleeth's Guide to the cello – knowing as I do that one would be hard put to find more sustained and inspired guidance.

Foreword
by Jacqueline du Pré

I have a vivid recollection of standing on William Pleeth's doorstep for the very first time. I was ten years old. As I pressed the bell I felt rather nervous, and yet strangely elated. We had never met before, although I had heard him play at a concert and been deeply moved. Now that I was actually to see him face to face I wondered what sort of a man he would be. Wonderful, like his playing? Or remote and aloof – very much the great artist – who would not have time or interest in his new child pupil? I need not have worried. His warm, welcoming personality soon put all my doubts at rest and, in that first hour, we managed to explore a lot of musical territory, and a lot about ourselves. It was the beginning of an extremely happy partnership, which grew spontaneously, and stayed with us, throughout the seven years we worked together as teacher and pupil; and it has developed into an enduring friendship.

If I were to try in a few words to say all that I have gained from those vital years, I think it is, perhaps, the realization that music making is a never ceasing process of change and progress. One never arrives at the perfect performance, but nevertheless draws increasing knowledge and insight, and enthusiasm, from every moment. This causes our relation to music to become practically the reason for our existence. William Pleeth's enthusiasm is absolutely boundless. And anyone who comes into contact with him and his teaching will be able to feed from his love for music which, after all, is one of the most rewarding human manifestations.

Editor's Foreword and Acknowledgements

The thoughts and ideas in this book were expressed by William Pleeth in discussions and working sessions over a period of several years. As anyone who has worked with him knows, William Pleeth combines exceptional ability on the cello with extraordinary insight into musical performance and the art and craft of playing the cello. It is rare to find a teacher with such uncommon perception and insight into all aspects of musical performance; but rarer still is one whose gift for language enables him to convey ideas and images which go far beyond the limitations of mere words. Thus, when the idea of compiling and editing his thoughts for a book in this series first arose, the primary task seemed to be one of not only retaining the content, but of finding a way to freeze into hard, cold print the freshness and vigour of language he brings to every musical and teaching situation.

The best approach seemed to be to tape discussions and working sessions so that the text for the book would be based as closely as possible on spontaneous reactions by the author to musical and/or cellistic problems as they arose in the course of talking or playing. Later, as it turned out, material from the original tapes became a mere springboard for further discussion and for expansion of ideas. The mind of William Pleeth is so fertile, and his passion for communicating ideas so great, that many volumes might easily have sprung from these sessions. Indeed, the greatest task was always one of finding ways to concentrate and condense vast amounts of knowledge and insight into a relatively short space. The decisions on what to leave out were always difficult ones and, I must admit, were never completely resolved to my own satisfaction.

Because William Pleeth's use of words is so closely bound up with the insights they convey, I have attempted to keep them exactly as he spoke them whenever possible. There are, I am aware, certain drawbacks to this approach; however, I have felt throughout that the insights thus provided outweigh the drawbacks. I hope that most readers will agree with this decision and will find in this book the same inspiration which those who have worked with William Pleeth first-hand have found – the new vistas he opens up are important not only for their value in cello playing, *per se*, but for their application to every other aspect of life as well.

It goes without saying that a book of this nature is rarely completed without the help and assistance of many individuals. As this book is no exception, I would like to thank those whose efforts were of particular help in bringing this book to completion. I owe a special debt of appreciation to Moore Parker for the countless varieties of assistance and support he provided in the early stages of preparation; to Margaret Pleeth, whose tireless arranging and re-arranging of schedules facilitated collaboration between the author and editor; and to Ferne Pyron, whose willingness to perform a variety of thankless tasks in the final stages made completion of this book possible.

I am also indebted to Halsey Stevens for his painstaking and sympathetic reading of the early and final drafts and for his many useful comments and recommendations; to Pauline Alderman for her valuable suggestions on the historical preface; and to Henry Birnbaum and Michael Whiffin, whose comments in the early stages of writing proved most helpful.

Finally, I would like to thank Jaqueline Wood and Brenda Cochran, whose willingness to type and re-type and re-type again helped carry the burden of work through the many drafts of the text; and Virginia Kron, who undertook much of the leg-work along the way. To all who have been associated with me throughout the preparation of this book I am most deeply grateful for the unfailing support and encouragement they have given.

Nona Pyron
London, December 1981

Author's Prologue

My dear Patrick,

I will be brief, for it may have come to your ears that I am a lover of the pen only when it is in another's hand. The habit of years of communicating through speech – not to mention hand gestures – seems to cause great rumbles of protest from pen and paper as words come from this first-time author's hand.

That this little boat has been kept on course is due only to the warmth and wisdom of the informative meetings with yourself, Eric Fenby, Penelope Hoare, Veronica Plastow, and Bob Knowles, whose help in the final stages has been invaluable. For you all, therefore, my admiration, gratitude, and friendship.

Of Nona Pyron's part in grooming this 'wordy child' I can only say that she is the truly great 'Nanny'. I had the use not only of her outstanding music library but also her ability with the camera for certain hand shots – the taking of many of these would have tried the patience of the hardiest expert! My appreciation and admiration of her skills, patience, understanding and boundless other qualities would make the list of 'thank-yous' very long indeed, so let me just say, Nona, that you have my deepest respect and warmest thanks.

The possibility that, through this book, I may be keeping a contact of friendship and music-making with all those gifted young students who have, at one time or another, come from near and far to study with me, gives a very special dimension to my dedication and joy in both playing and teaching the cello.

Part One

The Philosophy of Playing the Cello

Heaven forbid that I should try to explain what I mean in black and white – it is very much person to person. One uses suggestive methods in order to convey – whether it is a physical or whether it is an emotional idea that makes it happen.

One
Technique in Perspective

*The spirit of the music is the only thing which can rightfully
dictate physical action on the cello.*

'Technique', in its fullest sense, means discovering and
developing the physical means for bringing into existence
a piece of music. Thus it follows that technique *per se*
cannot exist apart from the music it is meant to serve.
People who think in terms of 'studying technique' have
made a very small world of technique. You cannot fully
learn technique, you can only learn the *basics* of technique
– *real* technique is something which only begins to take off
when it is caught up in a creative musical idea.

The music is the vehicle of technique. Once we are
hitched on to the musical and spiritual momentum of a
piece of music and use the music as a vehicle to lift our
technique and carry it into new realms, the possibilities for
technical progress and development become endless. The
more we enlarge our own spirits through the musical
inspiration of the great masters who have written for our
instrument, the more we are going to discover about our
technique and how to stretch it to portray the roles they
have created.

One fears that many students fail to look at their art and
craft enough from this point of view. They look at it,
perhaps unconsciously, from the viewpoint of their own
technical limitations (we all have them, of course) and then
try to push the music into *that* mould, instead of letting
the music beckon to their technique and stretch it beyond
its previous limitations. Yet how much vaster even the

sheer technical possibilities become when we let the music mould *us* – spiritually, intellectually, and craftwise.

This fanaticism about 'technique', this practising of 'technique' as an end in itself, worries me – it severs the thread between the physical means and the music and creates a separateness which is contrary to the nature of things. One would like to see the pursuit of 'technique' (the purely physical, mechanical action on the cello) married to a much wider and less fault-building type of practising: one would like to see students work with imagination and organization and a real understanding of the validity of the subtler issues.

'Oneness' in playing

How can a physical action have a separate existence from the emotion which brought it into being and which it is to reflect? I do not believe it can. However well-intentioned, a purely technical approach to mastery leads ultimately to a blocking of even technical fulfilment. And when the student tries to counteract this built-in limitation by practising even more 'technique', he finds himself caught up in a vicious circle where the 'oneness' of his playing is undermined: a wedge is driven ever deeper, splitting his creative force right down the centre. We simply cannot escape the fact that when we impose a technical separateness on our playing, we also impose a limitation which in the end will leave both the music and our technical and expressive powers unfulfilled.

The act of playing – physically and spiritually – must be one of relative balance and completeness in our whole being, for each aspect is carrying the other aspect and all must travel together along the same wavelength. Everything causes everything, everything gives birth to everything, everything feeds everything – the 'oneness' of you, your instrument and the music should be so perfect that all three marry into one entity in the end: one seamless whole in which one cannot see where the one part leaves off and the other begins. Whatever you are conveying musically, it has to have this perfect unity, because it is only when one has this kind of completeness that one can become a complete creative being.

This essential quality is all too rarely heard in cello playing at any level: one hears instead the opposing forces battling against each other – 'me versus my cello, and the two of us versus the music' – and cellists (all instrumentalists for that matter) often reduce themselves to that kind of battle when what they should be doing is not battling at all, but embracing and embodying all three aspects. There are many ways one can play a piece of music and still be 'right' in terms of what the composer has given, but in each case the 'oneness' of it must be there – out of sheer proper living together with oneself, the music and the cello.

At all levels of playing, from the very first lesson to the concert platform, this concept of 'oneness' has to be encouraged and cultivated to the point where it becomes one's second nature on the cello. Even when a child has his first lesson and the teacher plucks the strings to acquaint him with their sounds and names, this should be done in a way which will convey many suggestive moods and atmospheres and will stimulate his imagination and fantasy from the start. Thus in the first unconscious stages there will be engendered in the child's contact with the instrument a heightened awareness of the relation between physical action, sound, and an emotion or idea. From there he can be encouraged to go on and create new moods which have grown out of his imagination and, eventually, the music he begins to play. From that well-spring his unified growth on the instrument will continue throughout his musical life – and his approach to playing the cello will be one of *living* the music, not manipulating instrumental techniques.

'Living the music' means that all the various aspects – the cellist, his instrument and the music – come together in a perfect and mutually supportive union. If we mishandle the growth and development of any one aspect, then we shall undermine or even destroy the 'oneness' and produce something which is musically and cellistically still-born.

Gesture and emotion

Our heart has the most wonderful partner in our hands – their gestures are the outward expression of what we feel inside. Whenever we make a stroke with our bow, when we place a finger on a string, we cause a sensation of sound and feel; and the gesture of the bow and of the finger which brought that sound into existence must breathe with the life of the emotion that gave birth to it. Musicians must never let the fact that they have to master an instrumental craft cause them to lose this natural link-up between gesture and the feel for the whole drama and emotion of the music.

It is true, of course, that the nature of our craft is such that it is often necessary for us to analyse the physical movements we make in the act of playing, but we must understand that it is not the analysis that makes it happen in the first place. If you *live* an action, the feel of it in your hand (with the ear as your guide and master), you can analyse it later on if you want to. But never manufacture a movement out of an abstract analysis – there are too many other subtle factors at work.

A gesture does not normally precede the thought or emotion that generates it: we shrug our shoulders, we wave to a friend, we smile, we frown, and in every case the emotion comes first and the physical action responds as an expression of that emotion. We flick a duster because we want to flick a duster; we do not manufacture a movement in the hope that the flick of a duster will come out of it. Yet how often do cellists sit in the practice room trying to produce physical actions before they have even experienced the emotion which is suggestive of the physical action and which is its necessary counterpart! There is by nature a momentum of the one thing which carries the other. If the student can discover this and harness its

5

energies, he will learn how the spirit can feed the technique, and how the technique can carry the music on its shoulders.

The dangers of isolating 'science' in the investigation of technique

In some people there is a tremendous intellectual exclusiveness which prevents them from believing something unless they can first prove it to themselves in scientific terms. Many people have gone so far down the road of scientific investigation into physical action in cello playing that they have lost sight of any natural foundation for that action – and therefore any reliable foundation for their science. (By 'science' I mean the intellectual investigation into physical movement on the cello and the knowledge which is derived from that investigation.) Having developed theory before they have understanding, they have created an artificial basis for physical action which absolutely destroys natural action and ridicules nature.

If one looks for the science first in cello playing, instead of letting science grow out of the nature of physical action as it relates to the music, then the science will tend to become the end, the ultimate goal, and the music only a by-product. Physical movements arrived at in this way become set formulas and, in their isolation, are deprived of the nourishment which would allow them to flourish.

Of course we need formulas when we are first learning, but the basics of technique should be practised only in the understanding that they are going to be stretched and varied when they are incorporated within a bigger musical scheme. Formulas become dangerous when what should be a *basic* action becomes the ultimate and *only* action – a single remedy for however many varied situations one meets instead of the germ from which a wide variety of actions can grow (think of the hammered finger action one hears so often when the music is crying out for a thousand different finger treads). Through blind adherence to formulas, the theory of finger and joint action (in either hand)

6

can become so narrow and abstract that any potential musical variation that passes under its nose has to get down on its knees and become subservient to the artificial laws of that isolated, studied movement. Instead of uniting with the music and serving it, the techniques which this kind of science produces destroy the very heart of the music.

The sad irony is that the adoption of the scientific approach often comes about because the cellist is reaching out for greater perfection in his craft – reaching out in order to *serve* the very thing which his isolated science destroys. He does not understand that science on its own is always a very fallible thing – fallible because it is incomplete.

When science is isolated as an end in itself, that wonderful primitive thing called *instinct* withers before it is ever allowed to blossom into full maturity. *Unharnessed* instinct, of course, can present great dangers, but the proper use of science is to channel and train the instinct and thereby allow it to blossom with ever *greater* certainty – not kill it off. Only when science works together with nature and relates itself continuously to nature does it become a healthy basis upon which one can build. And only when both science and nature are caught up in the pull of musical instinct are they made complete; that is the force which draws them together into a unified whole.

Lack of recognition of the need for this, however, can cause people to erect walls that separate one aspect from another – and the reason I am so critical of isolated science in particular is because it is the most common cause of this division. Through the glorification of science as an end in itself, people tend to isolate it and treat it as if it were the foundation upon which all else rests. (*'You have to get your technique first.'*) But balance comes about only through the *non-self-conscious* involvement of science, for only then can there be a proper relationship between all the elements. In the greatest artists there is such a perfect fusion of science, nature and musical instinct that one loses any conscious awareness of them as separate entities.

7

The Cello

In the end one's playing should sound as unscientific and as uninhibited as the singing of a child's nanny who has not studied music but who will sit by the cradle and sing to the child with the most beautifully natural freedom. Whatever may be wrong with that kind of musical creation, there are basic things which are more right than what we do when we stifle and clutter our musical creation with so many scientific considerations that it loses all contact with the natural, instinctive expression.

Two
Completeness in Practising

People so often do not know what they are striving for in their practice. One should hunger after the whole concept, the whole mood, what the music stands for. That, to me, is being complete.

Of course students need to do their full quota of technical studies every morning (I think people often fail to do enough), but they should approach everything they do on the cello from an all-embracing point of view which does not exclude the musical vision. Even scales and studies should be caught up in some sort of a musical vision and feeling that lets them live. In the end, it all comes down to this matter of *balance* in one's practising—balance in the way one thinks about one's practising.

Balance means, for instance, that when we practise something slowly to ourselves we should be able to bring to it a slow-motion version of the spirit it is going to have later on. Even when we are practising slowly we cannot avoid playing with some sort of physical sensation in the left hand and bow arm; so why not, whilst we are feeding the note-learning into the brain, feed the right physical feels into the hands? Making something ugly just because one is *practising* destroys the balance, and it means that later on one is going to have to retrain one's hands and one's heart and make them relearn a whole new set of feels and sensitivities when one plays the same passage as a piece of music.

Prelude to practice

When you sit down in the morning to warm up on the cello, it should be in the healthiest and most complete way. Enjoy the simple beauty of the sensation of touching the cello and creating sound on it. Let your fingers and bow play around with complete freedom, following their own whim. Let them find their own way and they will eventually lead you to something – a scale or a study, or perhaps a passage from a sonata or concerto. From there on the music will give you your engine, your drawing power. Warming up should never be a matter of stale routine, but of allowing your mind and body and spirit the freedom to sense and discover what they (you) need. No two days need ever be the same.

The greatest value of this kind of warm-up is not only that your physical will warm up faster (using the word 'physical' as a noun to denote the physical aspect and involvement in playing, as I will use it in this book), but that your mind and musical sensitivity will not be shoved off into an isolated corner. Even five minutes with free play of fantasy will help you warm up the whole person, not just the fingers, and will bring *all* aspects of playing into touch with one another. Why should we shut out the musical mind and heart at any point along the way? They have to be harnessed to the physical action at some time, so why not from the very start? (There is in this approach to warming-up, incidentally, an ideal opportunity for beginning to toy with the idea of improvisation.)

It is worth mentioning in passing that Pablo Casals, by his own account, made a habit of beginning each day by first playing some Bach, to 'sanctify' the house, as he put it. I find this a wonderful idea, for not only does it sanctify the house, but it also sanctifies the mind: the spirit comes in touch with something marvellous and gives the physical something to ride on. It helps one draw a circle around, or through, the physical and spiritual aspects of one's being and playing so that there is a sense of completeness from the very start.

If you warm up in the right way, all your practising and playing will have a sense of completeness and integration. In the end it is not so much a matter of practising something, but of *living* in a complete way and *then* starting to practise.

Flexibility and imagination in practising

The very fact that students so often ask 'How should I practise?' is an indication that they have not been led from the start in the right direction of self-discovery, in the direction of understanding that there are developments in practising which grow out of progress, and that that progress in turn develops vision and the ability to break down problems. They look for an external 'system', a routine imposed from without, and because of this they go round in circles instead of upwards in an ever-increasing spiral.

Practising involves the understanding how one best uses nature – one's own nature and the nature of physical movement – in the process of enquiring into the physical means for achieving musical ends. By definition, this implies flexibility in the way one practises; and it is the opposite of that pre-set uniformity in practising which completely precludes any consideration for, or understanding of, the uniqueness of each individual, his temperament, his strengths and weaknesses.

Pre set uniformity in practising also tends to lead one into the habit of practising with a grim determination and battling on whatever the situation. Many people feel that unless they are battling with the cello (and themselves) they are not working properly. They get a guilt complex about not having 'practised'. It is an indication of how narrowly they have approached the whole question of practising as it relates to their being and their needs – and, for that matter, to their whole art.

The set practising routine may appear on the surface to

be more disciplined, but its discipline is only external. And, because it leaves no room for variation in the way one handles oneself, it therefore rules out any possibility of completeness in one's approach. It restricts and stultifies what should be an ever-growing and evolving mental and emotional agility. What one wants is not the limitations of the set routine, but the much broader and complete discipline of being able to work in a flexible way.

We have to understand and accept that there are no two temperaments alike – nor are the moods, dispositions and physical needs of any one person the same from one day to the next. One has to look inward first before one can relate to what is outside oneself: a person may be uninspired one day, or feel spent, or out of sorts, and it is pointless for him to set about practising on that kind of day with the same inflexible routine he would have on a 'good' day and then battle on even if nothing happens. (It is like getting your car stuck in the mud and sitting there with your foot still pressed against the accelerator, spinning your wheels, in the hope that the same techniques you used for normal road driving would somehow get you out).

Under different conditions we should be able to use ourselves completely differently. On an 'off' day in practising it might be by sitting back in a comfortable chair and learning the score, formulating the work in the imagination. Or it might be by mixing some score study with a bit of purified simple physical practice in a detached sort of way. There are many profitable ways one can use an 'off' day to prepare for and enhance the different kind of practising that will come on the next good day.

Flexibility and imagination in practising are not only important in determining the way we relate our practising to our own temperament and to our specific strengths and weaknesses; they are also essential in determining the way we relate the way we work to our own progress. We need to be able to recognize that while a certain type of practice, or a certain way of thinking about a passage, may have been necessary at a particular stage in our development, there comes a time when we should be able to leave it as that sort of effort and develop further ways of working on it that are in step with our own progress. It is a bit like feeding a baby: as the baby grows, its diet evolves to fit its changing needs.

The pursuit of technique in practising

There are two attitudes which, more than any others, tend to block students in their pursuit of technique in practising. The first is a **search for security**. Over the years I have heard many players with good run-around techniques still grinding away on a mechanical practising of the basics of technique, and I often ask myself what the driving force behind this kind of practising is. Is it fear that as a human being one might make a mistake? A fanatical search for security? If it is, then it is looking for a security that does not exist within the context of the human being. And while one is searching for that pot-of-gold-at-the-end-of-the-rainbow, one is destroying one's whole musical sensitivity and one's link between physical action and musical expression – and thereby one's best means of being relatively secure. The danger in this single-minded attempt to progress in the purely technical aspect of playing (to the exclusion of the musical) is that it begets its own kind of fear, which, in turn, requires more and more practice of the same sort to counteract the unnatural habits engendered by the fear – an unhealthy and unending circle.

The second attitude which is nearly always counter productive in the development of a real technique is a **greed for 'achievement'** in the most superficial sense of the word. Students often set off on this wrong path because they are searching for the most apparent and immediate type of success in technical progress. They develop, or are influenced by their teachers and colleagues to develop, a greed for superficial technical achievement. This engenders a mentality which imagines a kind of 'Olympics' for the cello in which measurable speed, loudness and certain kinds of agility overshadow or completely obliterate the subtler uses of the physical on the cello – uses which, incidentally, embrace and develop even *greater* speed and agility in the end. They fail to understand that the real test of speed or loudness (or whatever aspects of cello-playing one cares to name) is the *variation* of qualities that sit inside that speed or loudness. Speed for the sake of speed, or loudness for the sake of loudness, is not only superficial, but a musical *cul-de-sac*. When students are encouraged to focus their attention on the development of a *'technique'* (without being shown at the same time what the source of that technique should be), they will struggle after mechanical perfection on their instrument without any idea of what that mechanical aspect has to be attached to. Ultimately they find a wedge pushed between their feeling for the musical mood of a piece of music and the translation of it into sound via the cello.

The worst thing about this mentality is that it causes students to lose their healthy motivation towards an integration of their craft with their art. Following the carrot-in-front-of-the-nose promise of 'technical progress' (so-called), they are unwittingly led *away* from the life-giving aspect of their art so subtly that the two part company without the student ever knowing what is happening. The chain which should have bound everything together lies a clutter of useless broken links.

The inescapable fact is that one cannot pull a steel shutter down on the musical side of what one is doing because one thinks one is 'practising technique'. The feel, the mood, the sense of movement, the purity of sound, the spirit of the music – these are not things cut and dried which you later on attach to your technique. They are that which infuses every physical movement you make on the cello with life and spirit.

The technique and the music should work together like a team of horses pulling a coach, each perfectly in step with the other and each promoting confidence in the other. Whilst striving for the highest degree of perfection in both aspects, one must not let the 'horse of technique', out of fear for its own security, panic and bolt; nor must one let the 'musical/emotional horse' wallow in a self-satisfied indulgence that is oblivious to the fact that it is not technically fulfilled. The link between the two is the issue upon which life depends.

Destructive attitudes in practising

I remember a student playing the double-stop passage in the first movement of the Saint-Saëns Concerto. She played it accurately enough, but she sounded like a little automaton. 'You don't know how well your fingers know it,' I said; 'take your mind off your fingers and let's see where they take you when you let them go for a walk on their own.' Then I talked to her while she was playing the passage and made her talk to me; and, though she played it twice as quick as it ought to be, it was flawless – and the look on her face! I asked her to do it again at the right tempo, and said, 'Talk to me, look around, look at that picture,' and the delivery again was marvellous. She could have practised the other way until she was a little old lady of 98 and it would not have got any better. The first way she played it was accurate enough, but it was still-born; the other way was both accurate and brilliantly alive!

One has to find ways to deflect that kind of destructive or inhibitive interference and let the hands, once they have become familiar with the notes they have to play, go on their own. One of the best ways is to learn to distract oneself – look away, talk to someone, let it happen. It teaches one something about trust *and* about how one can undermine a passage with too much care and the wrong kind of determination. It also serves as a sort of therapy, an antidote to the type of fear one should have left behind as soon as the notes in the passage were mastered.

It seems so difficult for people who think they must consciously control every movement to switch off and let things find their own way. When they start to play the cello, the wrong emphasis on science causes them to become so preoccupied with themselves physically that they actually interfere with what should be natural actions. But look, for instance, at those fantastic gypsy fiddlers: their unstudied naturalness (in which science is allowed to have free play with instinct and nature) gives them greater technical facility than they could ever achieve from a determined and scientific approach to technical mastery. This is the kind of natural and instinctive mastery that those of us who pursue music as an art should develop as well. When I say to someone, 'Be reckless in that passage, be a devil and have a go', I am trying to destroy a bit of this self-conscious, over-calculating, determined 'technique' that goes so wrong when it comes face to face with the expressive content of the music – which, in fact, effectively *prevents* the player from ever coming face-to-face with the expressive content of the music. Being reckless a bit and getting on with your work, trusting a bit, flying blind a little bravely, are important to counteract an over-fearful, over-scientific attitude.

It is easy to manufacture worry about our playing; and then sit there waiting to pounce on what might go wrong, instead of having a tremendous sort of acceptance of what goes right. The wrong kind of determination can cause us to become so full of effort, so full of purpose, so full of scientific interference, that we never recognize when we would be better off having a *musical* 'interference'. The practice room is really the place just to sit and let it happen; what cellists have to push out of their minds is 'bad' playing; and start playing just for the love of it. This kind of acceptance is essential if we are to discover what state of fluency we have reached in the progress of a passage or work. The degree of interference on the part of the over-anxious player, through the habitual mentality of a 'rescue operation' for something which has not even taken place yet, often hides from him the discovery of just how fluent he may have become in a passage.

The important thing is that when we play we let

ourselves be carried in the right direction, so that we do not get a chance to become self-destructive. Even when we know it is going to go wrong, we should use ourselves as if it were going to be right (there is no reason why we cannot go wrong nicely). And when we do go wrong under those circumstances, it will tell us something about what went wrong in relation to a *healthy* physical action, not a frustrated, inhibited movement.

Three
Right Attitudes towards the Study Book

The study book is one of the most misunderstood and abused aids to technical development on the cello; there are those who scorn it, and those who make it the be-all and end-all of practising.

I personally want to defend the study book, but I want at the same time to criticize the limited way in which it is used. Through an unimaginative tunnel-vision approach to it, many people have let the study book entice them into using it wrongly. It is not merely something that presents a formulation of notes which then triggers in the cellist an appropriate series of physical movements; it is also an exercise for the mind of the student, an exercise in learning to unravel problems – in developing the means to unravel problems. The study book is something from which you extract knowledge.

Of course the study book does present note sequences which, on the most primitive level of understanding, require your hands to make certain movements. But what it does not give you – what it could never give you – is a deeper understanding of the wider implications those movements can have in relation to your specific needs and degree of technical development at a given time. Of necessity it talks on the surface, and the notes it gives you are surface notes; it is up to you to use your imagination to probe beneath the surface of the notes and discover the deeper subtleties that relate to your particular technical needs. You should think of the study book as a door through which you enter a great house. What you look for once you are inside and how you look for it is something which comes from you rather than from the study book. It is not enough just to knock on the door of each study and then push on to the next, telling yourself 'I've done that study'. Studies, if they are used in the right way, are there for life. It is your mind which has to take you beyond the façade and lead you to discover the deeper implications and possibilities for technical advancement in any formulation of notes.

You might, for example, have a study in legato playing: but if you do not ask yourself how you can use this study to strengthen your particular weaknesses, if you do not use your imagination and say, 'How many kinds of shifts can I learn from this?', 'What are the subtleties in the relation between the bow contact on the string and the movement of the left hand in these shifts?', if you do not notice that the move from one note to another within a legato can be a slide or a delicate shift, or a gentle binding between two notes, then you will not learn much from your study in legato playing. These questions all have to be self-asked. No one else can do it for you: they are what takes you through the door and into the house.

The breaking down of a study into numerous 'mini-studies' should be for the student like the working out of a puzzle. There are studies within studies within studies. There are studies within every single bar of a study! It is like the wheels within wheels you see when you open a watch: if you look more closely, you will see that each wheel is driving another. In a similar way each aspect of a study is linked with and driving some other aspect.

I would like to see more students develop the ability to find those 'wheels within wheels' and not just head always for the main wheel and let the matter drop there. There is no profit in fooling oneself that the quantity of studies 'done' is the measure of one's technical conquest. Students who work in this superficial way have not even begun to make a dent in the armour that is protecting them from their inadequacies – to which a particular study might provide a solution if they were to use it to greater advantage.

Once developed, the habit of breaking down passages into mini-studies will spill over in a valuable way into sonata and concerto practice: there are, for instance, as many studies in any single Baroque sonata as you will ever find in a study book. Students who say, 'Oh dear, I haven't done any *technique* this week because I've been practising my sonatas' have missed the point entirely. The potential studies they encounter in a sonata or concerto should provide a stimulus for them to extend those concepts which they have derived from the study book into situations where they will be clothed in a heightened emotional context and thereby lead to even subtler forms of technique. Nearly all technical problems exist in a more advanced and suggestive world of technique in almost any great piece of music. Through the music we can all expand our technique even further; and then, as our ideas as musicians grow, the way in which we use our technique will grow and change.

The study concerto

Because the study concerto has become a very neglected area of learning in recent years, and because it is, in its way, the ideal link between the study book and the real artistic repertoire, I feel that it is important that cello students once again become aware of it.

Study concertos are concertos written by cellists who, through their first-hand knowledge of the instrument, are able to indulge in a wide spectrum of techniques. All of the cellistics one encounters one by one in the study book are wrapped into a single, larger parcel in the study concerto and, though they are musically not on a level with the greater concertos, they provide a compendium of technical usage on the cello within a musical context.

Because of this, the study concerto is a marvellous 'stature-builder', physically and mentally. It does not matter that it is not great music; it is musical enough to incorporate all these cellistics and thread them with a musical spine, and it does provide the student with the means for enlarging his physical and emotional stature in preparation for later study of concertos of the calibre of Dvořák, Schumann, Elgar and others. The near death of the study concerto in modern practising is shutting out an important mid-way station in the student's learning, and is depriving him of an essential step in his development and a healthier, more consequential means of developing his technique.

It is worth mentioning finally another group of 'half-way house' concertos which are wonderful muscle- and stature-builders. These are the simpler concertos, written by non-cellist composers, which avoid the non-stop cellistics of the study concerto and do not make all the technical demands of the great performance concertos, but which have considerable musical merit. Concertos by Volkmann, D'Albert, Lindner, Raff and Molique come immediately to mind, but there are many more. We need works like these, as well as the simpler study concertos, because of the marvellous way they can begin to stretch the basics of technique towards a greater musical fulfilment.

Four
On the Life of the Left Hand

The complete freedom of the left hand to go wherever the music directs it – like the weathervane on top of the church that's so well oiled that it moves with the slightest breeze, nothing restricts it.

Think how beautiful the act of movement is, and what a marvellously satisfying thing it is to make any movement freely. Even the simple act of opening and closing the hand with a sense of response and a complete freedom of movement can be a wonderful sensation, a physical action so complete in its natural perfection that there is almost a spiritual feeling about it. One should hunger for the beauty of the sensation of movement, and the response of movement to what we think and feel.

The hand as the mirror of musical intention

How would you stroke a baby kitten or a little chick? Would it not be different from the way you would stroke a big, strong Alsatian? The love you feel might be the same, but your physical action would instinctively relate to the size and strength of the Alsatian or the gentleness and fragility of the kitten. Both gestures are equally valid but, because they relate to different worlds of touch and sensitivity, they are bound to be quite different in nature.

If we accept this kind of instinctive physical response in everything else we do in life, then surely we must realize that the sensation of physical movement on the cello is just as intimately bound up with response to emotional feelings –

or *should* be. It is the infinite variety of expression in music which demands from us a capacity for infinite variety of touch and feel in our hands: all our movements when we are playing should come as a spontaneous reflection of the emotions evoked by the music – and variation within movement should come as the natural result of the emotional variation within the music. Consider all the endless sensitivities of feel and tread that the left hand alone is going to have on its journey through a piece of music, the tremendous potential for variety in any single phrase. Imagine the endless variations of subtlety of touch and movement, the different ways of 'treading' the fingers can have. There must be hundreds, thousands – and each one coming as a *response*, a physical action evoked by something which is outside itself. It is *this* kind of logical movement of the left hand that we must learn to hunger for, and never let the knowledge that what we are doing is a highly developed craft tempt us into reducing the response of our hands to a limited number of pre-set movements.

The more the left hand knows its instrument, and has the freedom and flexibility to respond instinctively to the emotional demands of the music, the more perfectly it will be able to take on something of the life suggested to it by the music. This is the whole point: *the life of the hand in its many guises.* And this life depends for its existence upon freedom and release in the left hand. It is freedom we need to seek – freedom *of* movement, freedom *in* movement.

Freedom and independence of finger action

That is why I am so opposed to the set hand. The pre-positioned hand in cello playing cannot possibly respond to the music or reflect what we are feeling musically and emotionally: it is the greatest enemy of freedom in the left hand. What we want when we are playing is a feeling of *release*, of letting the fingers go.

I know that many cellists defend the practice of holding

the fingers down on the grounds that it gives the playing finger greater strength and security. But if one thinks further into the matter, one comes to see that this approach not only undermines the strength of contact by the playing finger, but also greatly restricts its potential for expressive variety.

Even pitch suffers from the limitations of the set hand. Most of the sour intonation one encounters in cellists who otherwise play well comes because they attempt to keep as many fingers as possible down while they are playing: in fact, many cultivate the habit in the belief that they will be able to measure the distance between two notes by the degree of stretch they feel in the fingers. I personally feel that this approach is very fallible, because the inevitable muscular tensions pulling the fingers this way and that will not only effectively prevent them from being truly in tune, but will also make it difficult, if not impossible, for the hand to relate and respond to the musical intention.

Measuring interval distance by the feel of tension between set fingers implies that one has no real understanding of the pitches on the fingerboard except relative to a finger which is already firmly placed; it is like groping in the dark and finding one's way across the room by reaching from one object to another. It also destroys, or at best stultifies, the feel for distance in movement and the aural sensation of distance which are an essential part of the beauty of the interval.

Pitch and interval relations are something which exist in the mind and the ear, and they must in the end become inseparable from our physical action. A pre-positioned hand will stubbornly maintain *its* right to dictate finger placement (and therefore pitch), and will therefore only inhibit the hand's natural ability to develop the sensitivity of 'fine tuning' which is essential to expressive playing. Good pitch is governed by much finer degrees than the set hand will allow. Suppleness and pliability of the left hand – release – is the essential starting point if the hand is to become, as it must become, the tool of the ear.

The released hand and 'fine tuning'

While *basic intonation* derives from a more or less logical division of the string into twelve notes within the octave, and is based on calculated finger action, *'fine tuning'* extends that basic concept to an infinite number of pitches within the octave and is based almost entirely on the aural sensation of distance. The fulfilment of the aural sensation of distance depends on the ability of the hand to respond in the finest and most minute way to the discrimination and anticipation of the ear.

Now I know that this view of intonation will seem strange to many cellists; we are all taught from the earliest lessons that the notes in the octave are distributed along the various strings in a more or less regularly spaced sequence, and we learn to place our fingers in a way that will enable them to stop the string at those places. But we should also realize at some point along the way that this way of playing relates only to basic, or approximate, intonation, that it is only a rough guide to help us get started.

If we do not understand this and we stay with the 'equal distribution' concept of intonation too long (or, worse yet, develop it into a theory or system of finger placement), then the hand is likely to become so set in its positions that it will take command over the ear and become the determiner of pitch. When that happens we are heading for disaster, or at least intonational mediocrity (which is a kind of musical disaster). The hand on its own is deaf and therefore can never rightly be the determiner of pitch. A preconceived placement of fingers according to mechanical and abstract principles only leads to the musical equivalent of 'painting by numbers'.

The translator of distance on the fingerboard is and must always be the *ear*. The ear is to the musician what the eye is to the sculptor: just as the eye guides the hands of the sculptor, so must the ear guide the hands of the musician. And just as the sculptor's eye can anticipate and react at one and the same time, so we must learn to use the ability of the ear not only to react to what the fingers have done, but to live the music (and the most refined intonation) almost as if it had heard it before it was played.

It is amazing how this approach to intonation reshuffles the left hand in its inner feel for the note. It is almost as if there were an 'ear' in the hand, an 'ear' that guides the fingers to where they need to be according to the harmony and texture around any given note. The ear, if it is properly used, is the guidance system – but, again, only a released and pliable left hand can react with a sense of unity and completeness to the information fed into it by the ear.

Fingerings and musical logic

Of course, it is important for cellists at the first stages of playing to learn their academic fingerings, for these provide a very good foundation for getting around on the fingerboard. But once the student has learned his basic fingerings and has understood their logic, he must then go on to learn and understand a *greater* logic, which is the logic imposed upon fingerings by the demands of the music. Academic fingerings are not the end of the road, they are a point of departure from which should branch out endless possibilities in order to fulfil the expressive subtleties of the music.

The endless possibilities include, I might add, the possibility of using those self-same academic fingerings one started out with. An excellent example of where an 'academic fingering' serves the music best, and yet for some reason is rarely used, occurs in the opening of the last movement of the Brahms F major Sonata:

One usually hears this played with fingerings that are fussy and busy, or sensuous, when all this passage is asking for is a fingering that will let it retain its simple, innocent, childlike nature. For this tune I find that the simplest academic fingering imaginable, beginning on either the thumb or first finger and staying in position, serves that purpose superbly.

Right or wrong, for it is not a matter of my personal opinion, the important thing is that the cellist has thought about the relationship of a fingering to what he sees as the musical demands of the passage.

Exploring new fingerings

A set, inflexible approach to fingering tends to build a wall between a cellist's musical intent and his physical realization of that intent. If he wants to get around that wall and allow the two aspects of his playing to begin to find each other, he can do so best by developing the boldness to explore the map of the countryside of his instrument until he finds fingerings which reflect whatever subtleties the music suggests to him – the mood, the colour, the sentiment.

There is, unfortunately, a dangerous kind of comfort or security which can creep into our approach to playing and affect our choice of fingerings: the security of accepting a fingering just because it is given in some edition. We must remember that when we see a fingering printed in the music it is only the editor's personal choice, and it may have been made for very personal reasons having to do with *his* hand, *his* musical training, *his* personal make-up, and *his* insight into the musical intent of the passage. It may be right for him, but is it for everyone? Your hand may be different from the editor's, or you may feel differently about the music; so it is up to you to investigate and not take an editorial fingering as gospel truth. You certainly have as much right to investigate, according to your musical insights and according to your hand. You may even agree in the end that the editor's fingering is the best for you; but only after you have investigated many other possibilities will you be in a position to evaluate his fingering at all.

It is not only the right of the cellist to explore fingerings, it is his *obligation* to do so. It is an attitude which should condition his thinking from the very beginning and continue throughout his lifetime with the instrument. Even in the early stages of playing students should be encouraged to break away from the printed fingerings and discover alternate fingering possibilities. Advanced players in particular need to do this in order to develop and maintain versatility in their fingering choices.

I personally think that cellists should make it a habit to practise as many possible fingerings as they can find for a given passage. In addition to versatility, it will help them develop the ability to evaluate the natural strengths or weaknesses of one fingering over another, or the suitability of one fingering over another for different expressive needs within the musical context. (It is actually essential to practise this way if we are to overcome the natural tendency to seek refuge in the comfort of established fingering patterns.) There are, of course, many bad fingerings for any passage, but there are usually several which are good, and it is advisable to play all the good ones whenever practising a passage in order to develop and maintain both physical and mental flexibility. By doing this we shall, through the accumulation of knowledge about how fingerings work in relation to various musical situations, develop the ability to discriminate in our choice of fingerings. At the same time we shall develop in ourselves much more possibility for spontaneous fingerings in performance. The greater the musical work, the greater the need for this approach.

The importance of release in thumb-position playing

Because cellists usually learn to play in thumb position by

pre-setting the fingers in a fixed octave formation, there is a strong tendency for them to continue to use the hand in this limited way long after any need for it is there. The very term 'thumb position' conjures up something so difficult in their minds that they cling to the set position they first learned as if it were their only security against the perils of high-position playing, and ultimately carry it over into all sorts of musical and technical spheres where it does not apply. In fact, the inflexibility this set position engenders in the hand often becomes so perniciously ingrained in the student that he is completely unaware of the limitations it imposes upon him – and thus unable to overcome them.

Whilst no one would deny that there is much to be gained from using the octave formation at the beginning as a general guide for orienting the hand, it is nevertheless essential that, once the hand has become familiar with where the notes lie, one should also sense that it is time to let go. Science has done its job, and now that hand and those fingers must live in a world of greater mobility and imagination of use so that they can have greater breadth of response to all the musical and technical situations they will encounter – and the freedom to give birth to the full resonance and beauty of all the notes. (The very inadaptability of the set position to different musical situations is precisely what proves it wrong!) The thumb is something which moves with the hand – it should be no more set in thumb position than it is in the lower positions. Nor, for that matter, should the hand and fingers be more set in relation to the thumb than they are otherwise.

There are, however, many situations in thumb position when the fingers should be able to move away from the thumb and then back to it again with the same marvellous freedom that a fan has in opening and closing. The thumb in this case, though it remains released, acts as a point of stabilization. An excellent illustration of this use of the thumb and hand occurs in the first movement of the Haydn D major Concerto, bars 38–9.

The Cello

As the photographs below illustrate, the hand can stretch out with the greatest ease to take in the high F ♯ and then link it in an almost vocalized way with the A ♯ which follows. Surely this use of the hand is much more aligned with the spirit of the music at this point than an approach which freezes the hand in a set thumb position and then moves the whole apparatus up and down the fingerboard like a slide-rule could ever be.

1

2

3

4

5

6

Freedom and flexibility of the fingers and hand in shifting

The fingers should be used in this same free and flexible
way when one is shifting from one position to another. I
have watched so many cellists do a simple leap to the
higher positions and have seen them land on the top note
with the thumb and all three fingers pressed tightly into an
octave formation. And I feel it is vitally necessary to
question the logic of this use of the hand: whether from
the point of view of the added friction that several fingers
against the string will set up in the shift, or from the point
of view of '*direct transmission*' (which is rendered impossible when the weight of the hand and fingers are distributed in this way), or from the point of view of *intonation*
(which can only suffer from the locked position of the
fingers).

Because the feel for distance in movement, and the variety of tensions which release in the left hand generates, are essential in the creation of good shifts, any attempts to shift with the hand held in a set position and the fingers pressed tightly against the fingerboard is bound to be one of the most counter-productive moves imaginable. If a cellist burdens his hand with a grip so tight that an enormous force of energy is required to dislodge it and shove it on to the new position, if he creates a situation of maximum tension in the hand (however unwittingly and unwillingly) and thereby reduces the hand to a minimum of mobility and sensitivity, then the intolerable demands of force and energy he has placed on his hand will make even the slightest change of position an awesome task – and any pursuit of responsive movement in the shift will be made difficult, if not impossible.

Subtleties of speed and 'feel' in shifting

Expressive variety in shifting is very much a matter of understanding the sentiment of the music and allowing the hand the freedom to move in relation to it. Thus the technique of shifting becomes really a question of how one approaches the mental and physical aspects of movement, for in shifts one should hear endless varieties of movement reflecting the endless subtleties within the music. Cellists should strive to develop within themselves a much wider and more imaginative attitude towards what is being asked of them in a shift – and recognize the relationship between this demand and their use of movement.

The various sentiments of the music are so vast that they can never be compressed into set formulas of movement which allow only a limited repertoire of movements in the shift – nor should the hand ever be allowed to become so set or rigid in its adherence to formulas of speed or formulated ideas of positioning that it cannot be responsive to this variety in the music. The very variety of expressive possibilities in the music should be like a light beckoning to the cellist, encouraging him on and drawing him towards ever-increasing exploration in the subtlety of movement on the cello.

Speed in shifts

The set and rigid hand is not the only enemy of expressive shifting, there are also attitudes towards the act of shifting which can reduce a cellist's scope for movement in shifts to a limited number of set formulas, thereby additionally robbing the music of its potential variety and subtlety. One attitude derives almost unconsciously from the fact that in the early stages of playing there is an urgency put in the cellist's mind to get from point A to point B. This is understandable and difficult to avoid because even when one first learns the scales one is bound to discover that between the smaller action of finger-to-finger there comes at times the larger action of the shift; this involves the movement of a much larger and relatively clumsier piece of mechanism (the arm), which nonetheless has to move with the same ease, speed and agility as the finger. Because of this there is from the start a slight panic element injected into the action of the shift. Add to this the additional panic caused by the distances a cellist has to cover in some shifts and, as time goes by, a way of thinking becomes embedded in the student's mind which leads him to strive for maximum speed in every shift, obsessed with only the one single thought of 'getting there'.

Now it is true that on a big instrument like the cello the sheer distance of a shift does tend to exaggerate the sense of movement in speed; but because of this it is all the more necessary for cellists to fight the compulsion to move at maximum speed in every shift – to do so will greatly narrow the expressive potential of the shift. A very fast shift can, of course, be expressive in music when it is appropriate, but other sentiments in music will dictate other speeds and qualities of shift. It is this great variety that the cellist has to be aware of and be able to relate his physical movement to. Ultimately it is the *emotional* measurement and the *emotional* sense of timing that should command the speed of movement in a shift.

Emotional speed in shifts

When I say to a pupil, 'Take your time in the shift', I am not suggesting that he should be careless about the rhythm. I am talking about the mental speed of the shift, the emotional energy behind the shift. I am trying to get him to avoid the trap of letting the brain race ahead as if it were frantically trying to make sure that the finger kept its appointment with the note, and to encourage him instead to concentrate on harnessing his physical action to the emotional feel of the timing as dictated by the music at that point. For example, in a relaxed passage he should allow his shift to be pregnant with a laziness in the way it moves from point A to point B, whereas in a brilliant passage the shift will have to have the energy necessary to reflect the vivacity of that kind of music. One cannot say it often enough: every musical sentiment must have its physical counterpart.

If the energy and speed of a shift is divorced from the influence of the spirit of the music, it will be out of step with the emotion inherent in the music. It makes little difference whether the out-of-stepness comes about because the player has always practised his shifts as separate and independent physical movements, or whether it comes from an ingrained habit of always shifting at maximum speed (or a combination of the two), the result will be the same and the potential expressiveness of the music will be lost.

Tension and release in shifting

A student may know that 'sameness' in shifts robs the music of its potential for expressive variety, and yet not know where to begin to create shifts that can respond to the music's endless variation of moods, feel, senses of speed, weight, lightness. Variety in shifts is created through a subtle balancing of tension and release, but it is a delicate balance and can only be fully achieved if one begins from a point of maximum *release*, not maximum tension.

Just as it is release in the hand which allows it to be responsive to the musical mind and ear, it is release in both the hand and arm which provides the foundation for variety and subtlety in shifting; release is the starting point for all shifts. With a released hand it is easy to inject whatever degree of tension one needs into a shift, but if one starts from a point of maximum tension, it will be extremely difficult to 'inject' release into the tension and achieve the balance one needs in a shift.

Talking about release, however, is often easier than actually doing it, and students who have developed the habit of constant tension in shifts may find it difficult even to imagine what the kind of release I am talking about actually feels like in the hand and arm. Rather than expend more words on something which really has to be felt as a sensation, let me instead suggest an experiment which will give the reader a chance to feel this sensation for himself. Take your bow or any stick in either hand and hold it so that it is perpendicular to the floor (see illustrations overleaf). Then release your hand and allow the bow to slip through your fingers, and then catch it again a bit further down. (For safety's sake, try this experiment over a soft carpet). It slips through your fingers because you are *releasing* – and this is the sensation that you want to have in your shifts on the cello.

Of course, in real shifts the situation is reversed and it is the hand which moves along the fingerboard, but the sensation is the same: one should have the same feeling of letting the fingerboard slip through the fingers and then recatching it later on that one had in the experiment with the bow. It is a movement of unfettered lightness, and because it contains within itself (as a movement) the potential for unlimited variation in one's use of the hand

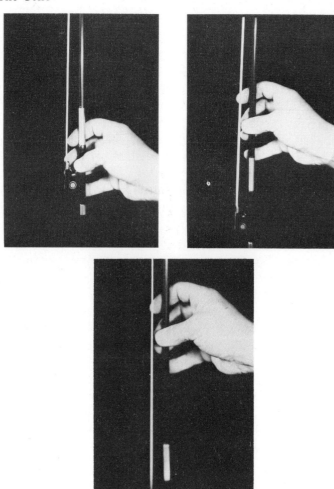

Experiment to illustrate the sensation of 'release' in shifting

and arm in shifts, it proves itself to be the starting point for all shifts.

In music with delicate fragrant moods where one wants no tension at all, the hand and arm will be able to release so completely that they will almost seem to float up and down the fingerboard; then from there the tension can be increased to any degree the music requires, all the way to shifts of the most passionate emotional intensity.

I have been stressing particularly the need for beginning from release because every cellist knows how easy it is, out of habit and training, and for the reasons we have just discussed, to allow maximum tension to govern our movement in a shift, and how difficult it is from that point to achieve any kind of balance or control in the shift. Yet, as we have just seen, it is upon this balance that control and subtlety in shifting depends. Even if one has just left a note which, for musical reasons, required maximum tension and is moving to another note of maximum tension, that tension must not carry through into the shift (except on those occasions when the cellist decides, for musical reasons, that it should). With the ability to release as a starting point in shifts, the cellist will be able to achieve not only the extremes of tension or delicacy in shifting but also every degree between.

Tension and release in slides

Excessive tension is not only a bad foundation for clean shifts, but it also destroys the possibility of control over the linking of two notes – or what we commonly call a 'slide'. If one listens to fine singers, one cannot help but be moved by the way they link notes; often the connection is so subtle that it is more implied than a reality. How delicate these tiny vocalized links often are – like a piece of thread through a row of beads; it is something you can almost *feel* rather than hear. There is a vast difference between this and *sliding* up to a note.

If we were also great singers and could sing our music, we would discover (perhaps to our surprise) the degree to which the move between the notes is only a binding factor, and that it is the notes themselves which must receive the emotional stress. We would then understand more clearly that a slide should rarely make itself more obvious as a sensation than the notes at either end. It is the notes that give birth to the slide, and not the other way round.

(There are, of course, slides – deliberately created

37

glissandi which are called for by the composer or are implicit in the nature of the music – which require an intensification of the sound between the notes. But this is a special case and a relatively rare occurrence, and we must not carry this technique, however valid in its proper context, into the other areas where the slide should be only a connecting factor.)

In the final analysis, the physical sensation of a shift, with or without a slide, is an *experience*, it is something your heart feels. You can never manufacture a physical action in the hope of contriving a musical idea: *musically* it will not work. Nor can you create good shifts without an unfettered physical action which allows the musical and emotional vision to take command. Allow yourself to be inspired by that vision, and you will then be in a position to discover all the subtle shadings of musical feeling which bring about the endlessness of the technique of shifting.

Five
The Marriage between the
Left and Right Hands

A perfectly balanced relationship between the hands is essential if one's playing is going to be an integrated and creative act.

It is the marriage between the sound production in our right hand and the colour production in our left that we are after. A perfect marriage: they understand one another, they relate to one another, they feed one another – they live together. Achieving this union between the hands depends upon our understanding the ways in which the hands have to work together and, at the same time, the ways in which they have to be independent of one another.

Independence of hand tensions

In cello playing there are not only basic differences of movement between the two hands, but also independent tensions needed for each hand. Think of a toddler going out for a walk with its father: although they walk side-by-side, each is using his legs quite differently in order to progress at that same pace, and the tensions in the two sets of legs, to achieve the same pace, will have to be quite different. In cello playing the principle is similar: if the two hands are going to 'walk abreast', as it were, then each is going to have to use itself quite differently from the other.

Both hands may have a maximum tension at any point in the music, but the maximum of each is an *independent* maximum, and if we make the mistake of trying to equalize the independent tensions wrongly, then we are going to take a very wrong path. A common example of this kind of wrong equalization occurs when cellists forget that the potential for dynamic power is much greater in the right hand than in the left. When the music grows louder, and becomes emotionally more intense, the tension in the right hand (necessarily) mounts with it; but if one makes the mistake of trying to match that necessary tension with an equivalent degree in the left hand, then the left hand will find itself saddled with more tension than is appropriate for its job and the strain of this will actually be detrimental to the work it has to do.

When we step away from the cello, of course, it becomes obvious to us that while more power in the right hand *will* increase the dynamic level, more power in the left can have no effect on loudness at all. A strong player might eventually be able to make dents in the fingerboard by using his left hand to maximum power, but for all his effort it would not make the music sound louder! (This particular misplacement of tensions may be one of the sources of the indiscriminate use of the wide vibrato – i.e., the left hand, seduced into trying to match the energy of the right, cannot go *into* the string any more, so it uses its energy to go sideways.)

If we do not recognize and accept that our left and right hands are doing different jobs (and that those jobs imply an imbalance in our use of them), we will not only be lured into trying to use them with equal tension, but will also prevent ourselves from discovering what has to be done in order that each hand may have the right amount of tension within the framework of its function. It is a tremendous discipline at times to keep the hands independent in their power, but in our craft and art it is essential.

The advantageous influence of the hands upon each other

The task of the player is not only to prevent the intrusion of harmful influences but also to learn when it is to his advantage to give way to such an influence. In order to do this, the mind must keep the whole canvas in view, even in the learning stages of a piece, so that the physical emotions in both hands can be trained to walk side-by-side.

There will always be occasions in which the technical command of the one hand is ahead of the other. When these situations arise and the hands get out of step with each other, one should try to discover which is the stronger partner in this particular case (not necessarily stronger in strength, but in command) and let that one lead the other. There are times, for instance, when the right hand can be so strong and self-assured that the left will be able to master its problems better by fitting itself *inside* the frame provided by the stronger right. In that case, let the right hand take the left hand for a walk. But at other times it can be the opposite way round, when the left is the stronger partner (for some reason people find this more difficult to spot and they often struggle to make their fingers play evenly without realizing that it is the bow that is chaotic), and then it is the left which must lead the right. Ultimately, if the hands are not allowed to serve one another, they will only diminish each other by getting in each other's way.

In the long run most cellists will discover that neither hand is necessarily weaker or stronger than the other – it is only that their jobs make different demands on them at different times. The important thing is to let the influence between the hands flow in the right direction so that the stronger partner is never dragged down to the level of the weaker and made to dance to its tune.

Mutual assistance between the hands becomes particularly important in shifts, especially the long ones. We talked earlier about the use of the left hand in shifts, but the life and sensitivity of a shift is equally dependent upon a fluid approach to the handling of the bow. As the left hand moves from point A to point B, the fine shading of the bow must render the movement of the left hand, and even the very shading of the bow itself, imperceptible.

This is something we do quite naturally in singing (even

the unschooled singing of most cellists!) As we sing an interval, we release the vocal cords, so that all the notes in between do not sound, while at the same time giving the illusion of continuity between two notes which are perhaps quite distant from one another. Why should our use of the cello's 'vocal cords' (i.e. strings) be any different? We should be able to give the illusion of continuity at any level of speed or dynamic, the right hand having the capacity for unending shading which perfectly matches and sustains the tread and sense of movement of the left hand as it shifts. After all, if we can separate one note from another on the same bow, and we can slur one note to another, then we should be able to shade to any degree between those extremes. It is a matter between the right hand on the bow and the left hand on the string.

False emphasis on the left hand

It is all too easy to let our fear of missing notes in the left hand spill over into the right and cause the sound to dry up, or to concentrate so heavily on note-hitting that our sound becomes still-born. But even in passages that are extremely difficult or tricky for the left hand, the right hand must be left alone to do its own job just as it would have done it under perfect conditions of the left (by working in this way the right hand will actually help the left hand in its work). We must never allow the expressiveness of our sound in the right hand to be destroyed or interfered with just because the left hand has not yet achieved its objective in commanding the difficulty of a passage (or because the left hand, having finally commanded it, remains preoccupied with a residual apprehension).

The perfect working together of the two hands is often undermined because cellists can become so preoccupied with the activities of the left hand that they neglect their sound in the right. It may be that the fixation many cellists have with finger action of the left hand comes from the association many musicians have with the piano, where the action of the fingers does indeed create the sound. But it makes little sense to carry this kind of thinking over on to the cello, where finger action does not create the sound but only *modifies* the sound created by the right hand. Cellists need to relate their thinking more to the craft of the wind instrument player (substituting 'bow' for 'blow'). Thinking in this way will put the relationship of the hands in better perspective.

Proper use of the bow will always result in scope for greater expressiveness in the left hand; and proper use of the left hand will let that expressiveness sit within the life of the sound created by the bow. In the final analysis it is the expressiveness of the right hand and arm, through the bow, which will open up the doors for the left hand. The *sound* has to live first.

The Craft of the Bow

Your bow is your voice – let it speak!

On superficial consideration the bow may seem to have a relatively easy job; but within that deceptively simple world of forward and backward movement there is a wealth of expressive power, and it needs a wealth of techniques to create it. The development of these techniques begins with our attitudes towards the bow and bowing. The sound we produce with the bow is the foundation for all else that happens on the cello.

Let the sound breathe

Have you ever blown soap bubbles through one of those bubble rings that children have? That simple act is to me almost a spiritual experience. You do not calculate before-hand that you are going to blow with x pounds pressure at y speed. You sense by instinct how gently or forcefully to let the air flow from your lips and lungs in order to create the bubbles and expand them without bursting them. The way you blow is something that exists in your imagination, something you can almost sense and feel before it happens.

When you think of your bow arm, think of air and of breathing. Use your right arm to create sound the way a wind player uses his lungs and breath, and use your wrist and fingers the way he uses his tongue and lips. It may seem strange to ask cellists to think of their bow arms and hands in this way, but the analogy is an important one; there is in string playing a natural flow of 'air' perfectly related to and regulated by the needs of the sound at any given moment in the music. It is the feeling of this flow of 'air' through your arm that you want to have as an actual physical sensation. When you have that sensation, you will be able to distribute the 'air', and modify it, in the same way a fine singer or wind player does with real air – and you will at the same time develop a sense of complete freedom in the right arm.

We need this sense of freedom in every bowing situation. You do not have to use the whole bow to be free, but within whatever dimension of stroke you are using at the moment the sound must have that same sensation of the freedom of the open throat, of the free flow of air through an unrestricted passageway. Even quiet passages require this same approach. Never imagine that smaller playing needs greater restriction of the bow: on the contrary, if it is going to be expressive, it will need to have relatively more freedom. (The very nature of smallness tends to entice us into becoming more restricted – into letting its restriction restrict us – and we have to counteract that consciously by having more abandon in our bow and in our sound, and learning to be very free within even a small world of sound.)

Tension and release in bowing

Try moving your finger back and forth across a smooth surface. Start with long slow strokes and then build up speed and let the strokes become quicker and quicker. You will discover that as you get quicker you will automatically lighten your stroke in order to prevent the increased friction from building up and starting to burn. This same principle can be applied to bowing strokes. The amount of pressure you put on the bow must always be related to the speed of the bow: the quicker the speed of the bow, the lighter the stroke must become, otherwise the tension will multiply itself to disproportionate degrees.

In passages of loud, fast notes the accumulation of

pressure in the bow as we go faster can grind the sound into the string and make it go dead – this is particularly true when the fast notes require separate bows. To counteract this we have to open out the bow and let more 'air' in – the faster and louder the notes are the more room they need to breathe. Power is never a matter of grinding the bow into the string, but of knowing at what point to release in order to create a balance between pressure and speed – between tension and release.

There are many musical situations, on the other hand, which require greater tension in proportion to release, times when we need to move with a slow, burning bow and yet let the bow travel with a sense of inner release. These are times when we need to have tremendous tension *inside* the sound whilst having at the same time the sense of thrust which comes from release.

This is a sensation we all know from experience. Any schoolboy or girl who has ever shot beans through a straw knows how to release pent-up tension to create thrust. And anyone who has ever flown in a plane knows the sensation of the pilot holding back the plane with the brakes whilst at the same time revving up the engines to push against those brakes, and how, when he eases the brake off, the release of that pent-up tension sends the plane surging forward. The archer, too, knows how, at the moment of greatest tension, to release the string and send the arrow flying. And we all know how, in driving a car, to nurse the clutch against the accelerator, holding the car back and accelerating at the same time, with an absolute sense of opposites within our power. These are living sensations, these opposites which sit inside one another, and we seem almost to have an instinct for enjoying them as pure sensation.

We need to have the same instincts and the same love of sensation on the cello. We must not let this side of our nature become dormant just because we think we are playing a musical instrument; only the means are different, but the instinct and sensation should be just as natural and just as enjoyable. Whether the release of tension is as gentle as a sigh or as continuous as a slow-flowing river, or whether it explodes like a shot out of a gun, it always has its own logic of being born.

Tension and release related to the up-bow and down-bow

Command over tension and release in bowing requires an understanding of the different properties of the up-bow and down-bow in string playing. Because the down-bow has an immediate sense of brute force (and therefore gives the illusion of power), people often get side-tracked into believing that it is stronger than the up-bow; they feel that in order to have a strong attack they need to use a down-bow. Yet the up-bow can often have the same sharpness and strength of attack, plus the added advantage of a sense of thrust and movement forward.

The sensation of strength in the down-bow comes because of the direct application of the weight of the arm and hand over the point of contact. But this belly-flop splash can often be so great that it creates an imbalance between the force of the downward attack and the forward flow immediately afterwards, making a continuity of movement and sound difficult. The up-bow on the other hand has an almost built-in balance between the force of the attack and the subsequent movement forward, because it starts at a point *away* from the hand and arm and plays into that weight. Since the movement forward sits in the lap of the attack, the notes can have greater stature.

The down-bow is, of course, no less wonderful when it is fulfilled in its own way – and command in bowing demands of us the ability to create equal sounds when moving in opposite directions – but I stress the up-bow here particularly because I feel that its potential is too often ignored by cellists. I personally find the up-bow a most marvellous gesture forward, like threading something into something. It gives the most wonderful sensation of pent-up power, like when you fence and thrust; and, in more controlled states of playing, a spell-binding sense of forward flow of movement.

Command in bowing

In general, cellists need to give a great deal of thought to the properties of the bow in the execution of different strokes. There are times when we shall want to draw upon those built-in properties and utilize them, and there are times when we shall need to equalize them and obliterate the differences (that is where our craft comes in). We begin to do this by first recognizing the very real differences in the bow between the frog and the point, and learning to develop techniques which can both utilize and counterbalance them.

Because musical considerations do not always give us a choice, we must be able to execute any stroke perfectly on either an up-bow or a down-bow. If we fall into the lazy habit of always adopting the most convenient manner of stroke (say, always using the down-bow for an attack), then we will never explore and develop the techniques for achieving the same stroke by other means. Yet when they are developed and handled properly, both up-bows and down-bows can attain an equal stature – it is only the means of producing the stroke that is different. One's command should, in the end, leave one free to choose the direction of the bow according to the more subtle requirements of the music.

How many cellists, for instance, have considered the possibility of beginning this passage from the Schumann Concerto with a down-bow?

Schumann, Concerto in A minor, first movement, bars 68–72

Not every cellist may share my preference for this bowing, but he should at least give some consideration to the advantage of forward flow into the top note after a sharp up-bow attack. It is not sufficient in our art to reject something on pure theory or habit alone; we should be constantly exploring and searching for technical means which will give better realization to the music. Each cellist will find his own solutions in relation to the music as he sees it, but these solutions can have real significance only if they are the result of wide-ranging thought and exploration.

There are, of course, passages which, for purely physical reasons, are more practical to execute in one bow direction than in another. In the last movement of the Haydn D major Concerto, for example (in bars 123–5, cited below), the bow movements have a natural ease if one begins with an up-bow. (In this case, and many like it, the economy of the up-bow, with its turning across the strings matching the curvature of the bridge, makes it easy to execute and makes the down-bow version seem clumsy and awkward by comparison. If one were to begin with a down-bow, then one would be moving counter to the bridge curvature and this would necessitate much greater arm movement – both along the path of the bow and in the up and down movement.)

But compelling physical reasons for the use of a particular bow direction do not occur as often as people think, and we are all too prone to relate the 'rightness' of an up-bow or down-bow to the degree of habit we have established through our practising of it. Once a habit becomes ingrained, then even very simple bowings can become uncomfortable when we have to turn them around.

Therefore we need from time to time to remind ourselves that we have been playing up-bows and down-bows ever since we started playing the cello (there are, after all, only two basic directions in which the bow can travel), and most cellists know how to articulate a note, or shade a note, or re-establish articulation between notes, or breathe between notes on either an up-bow or a down-bow. It is only habit that often fights our sense of comfort. But if we can learn to think purely in an expressive way with the bow, making full use of a free right arm, then that uncomfortable feeling of a 'wrong bow' will hardly ever exist for us.

On legato bowings

There is by nature so much spring in the bow when it meets the string, that it is our legato, not spiccato, bowing we have to cultivate. Our general law of bowing with the modern bow should be: if the bow is not made to sing *into* the string it will, being elastic by nature, want to leave the string. Thus, instead of worrying about how to bounce the bow, we should rather concern ourselves with what we have to do to *stop* the bow from bouncing.

It is this natural bounce we have to counteract when we play legato, and it is the pressure of the first finger of the right hand against the stick which regulates the degree to which the bow will sing into the string (or leave it). If a cellist is sensitive to the nature of the bow, he will let it tell him just how much pressure he is going to need with the first finger to hold it beautifully into the string. By starting in this way the cellist can then discover how to use himself *vis-à-vis* the natural properties of the bow to create all the many degrees of legato he is going to need in playing.

Variety within legato strokes

Variety within the legato stroke is something I find lacking in most cellists. Cellists on the whole tend to view legato as a narrow term and, depending on their habit, either play legato with a very smooth, unarticulated bow, or with a mannered 'huh-huh-huh' articulation everywhere. But whichever path they follow, it remains a very narrow approach to a type of bowing which should have the potential for immense variety. A fine pianist, by comparison, will have many varying degrees of articulation within the concept of legato. Admittedly, the very nature of their instrument causes them to give much more thought and consideration to this subject than string players generally feel they need to. But, by the same token, string players should not let the natural ability of their instrument to connect notes smoothly within a single bow blind them to the many possibilities of expressive fulfilment which are open to them within the concept of legato. Cellists can create even more types of legato than the pianist, so why just rest the bow on the string and pull?

Spiccato bowings

Now when we want the bow to leave the string, then our handling of it becomes a different matter: we will cease to oppose its nature and allow its natural elasticity to come to meet us in the creation of a spiccato bowing. The nature of the bow is to bounce. The role of the cellist is to support that nature and to channel the spiccato articulations into the right degree of length and height, of hardness or lightness, or whatever quality the music requires.

Thus it follows that our first task in spiccato bowing is to enquire into the nature of the bow's own ability to bounce *before* we decide what physical actions we need to add to make it happen in the right manner and to the right degree. Too much wilful control on the part of the cellist will cause the bow to lose its wonderful buoyancy, too many pre-formulated ideas of physical movement in spiccato playing will fight against the nature of the bow, too much determination to make it happen or keep it going will cause the wrist and fingers to tighten and all the brilliancy of the natural bounce will be lost.

The use of fingers, wrist and arm in bowing

The proper use of the fingers and wrist is important in every aspect of bowing; yet it is often difficult for those of us who play string instruments, because the nature of our craft requires us to give considerable thought to the movement and action of the wrist and fingers, not to become overly obsessed with them and develop ways of using them which are unnatural and mannered. When we write, for instance, the finger joints and wrist co-ordinate in a perfect sequence of interrelated movements. If we write very large (on a blackboard, say) the whole of the arm will come into use as well, whereas in the smallest writing the movements are pared down, many being left out altogether and new and more refined ones, which were not needed for the large writing, coming into play.

The way we use our fingers, wrists and arms when we paint a wall or a piece of furniture is another example of a beautiful, unconscious use of the joints and muscles involved – one which is very close to the movements we use in bowing. The next time you paint something (or watch someone painting) observe the natural interplay between the various parts of the fingers, wrist and arm. There is both perfection and logic in the way each movement carries through the various joints and muscles as the hand moves back and forth in its stroke, each one carrying on where the previous one left off. And yet, in all its perfection, it is not something which any one of us has to be taught.

But when it comes to playing the cello there seems to be a desire to erect barriers between ourselves and our natural movements. Perhaps this is because we know from the start that what we are attempting to do is a highly developed craft – and that knowledge forces upon us (wrongly, but inevitably) a negative sort of mentality in the way we look at what we are doing. (Unfortunately, many people go on to build their 'techniques' out of those barriers, unaware that they exist and are self-built.)

Yet it is the barriers themselves (often posing as solutions) which we must learn to break down and destroy. The best way to begin is to allow our muscles and joints to move with their own natural and primitive freedom, letting them get on with what they have to do free from any inhibiting considerations of 'how' on our part. Only from that basis can we begin to build a more healthy type of action.

When I explain this to students, they often ask me just how free they ought to be in the movements of their fingers, wrist and arm. The answer lies, however, not in the degree, but in the way we approach it. So I often answer by saying, 'You have in each leg joints at the hip, knee, ankle and toes; now when you walk out of this room do you plan to calculate beforehand just how those joints are going to work in relation to one another – how loose or how free they need to be?' It is the restrictive attitudes of the mind and intellect that destroy the basic naturalness of movement and make what we do on the cello artificial. 'Primitive freedom' is not floppiness and lack of control, it is simply the freedom of the body to act and react in a natural way. It is that kind of freedom we have to begin with before we can start to refine it and hone it to the requirements of our craft.

Sensitivity in bowing

The next time you walk over rough ground notice how your foot and leg muscles automatically accommodate to the changing terrain underfoot. Or notice some time how pliable people's faces become when they speak, as they reflect the emotions behind the words they are saying. Now apply this to the grip of the hand on the bow: should it not have the same kind of pliability and flexibility as it traverses the varied emotional terrain of the music, the same kind of instinctive reaction to the subtlety of change? The greatest enemy of sensitivity and subtlety of touch in the bow hand (and therefore in the sound it produces) is an unvaried and inflexible grip on the bow. There are no two moments alike for the bow, so why should the bow hand have one inflexible grip?

When you play, try to imagine that your right hand and fingertips are moving over the contours of the music in the same way that a blind person feels an object with his hands and fingertips. His fingers are not stiff and inflexible, imposing their will on the object to be felt, but rather gentle and sensitive, searching out the truth of its shape, letting the object guide the fingers. By sensitively following the contours of an object with his fingers, a blind person is able to recreate that object in his mind's eye. Even sighted people still use their hands to inform them about the shape of things; and if something is beautiful, it is almost an instinct to want to touch it and let its contours guide the hand. It is this quality of touch and sensitivity that cellists need to develop in their playing. Whether in a musical line of the utmost grace and delicacy, or whether in brutal music with heavy jagged lines, every mood, every curve in the line of the music is a shape which your bow hand should be following, a shape which will guide your bow and determine the way you use it to recreate its contours in sound.

Bowing strokes

One really cannot talk about bowing strokes on paper. This is where the textbook breaks down, because it cannot demonstrate a sensation. Of course one's first task in learning to play the cello is to assimilate fully the bowing strokes and techniques that are given in the textbook, but once one has achieved that command, then at every turn in playing one should be inventing strokes which are not in the textbook, strokes which go *beyond* the textbook, in order to meet the needs of the music. The textbook can only explain the basics – that this or that bowing is done detaché in the lower or upper half of the bow, and that it is heavy or light. It cannot convey a physical sensation that is linked to a mood or feeling; and that, ultimately, is what bowing is all about.

The world of bow usage is an unending world of change; it is a whole art in itself. But ultimately it is the musical art that is going to make you search out the technical means – strokes you will not be able to find in any textbook. How can the textbook show you that the same stroke can be soft and gentle, stern, brutal, or fanciful? Only the music can show you that. Whenever you are playing, visualize first the character you want and *then* find the means for achieving it with your stroke. The variations of any stroke must be endless.

Gesture in bowing strokes

For an artist every stroke of his pen or brush is a gesture which corresponds to an image within his artistic imagination, and cellists must develop a similar relationship in their use of the bow. Even those of us who are not artists still recognize the relation between what we think or feel and the marks we make on paper; whether we are drawing, writing or just doodling, whatever movement we make with our hand will have its visual counterpart on the paper, and we are in no doubt about the direct link-up between the thought, the movement and the visual result. It is a simple chain of events: what we think, we will do; and what we do, we will see.

When we play the cello, our bow is our pen, our brush; the only difference is that the marks it makes are aural, not visual. But the link-up between the heart, the mind, the physical gesture and the end result in sound is exactly the same; we cannot escape the fact that what we do we will hear. We cannot have right aural results if we do not make the right physical movements, because it is movement, it is gesture, which creates sound on the cello. Thought, action, sound, they are all different aspects of the same thing. The gesture comes about because of the temper of the mind or heart or spirit; and the sound comes about because of the gesture. As with the left hand in its own way, the physical action is the mirror of the spiritual feeling or intent. It is absolutely up to your heart to govern, and for the right physical action of the bow to follow. *This* is the craft of being expressive from the right hand.

Expression, breathing and articulation in bowing

We are all used to being expressive when we talk. Nobody tells us what to do, how to separate one group of words from another or where to breathe for emphasis and clarity in meaning, but we do it just the same and it all seems very natural. The beautiful thing about speech is that the timing of it, the way we use our breathing in it, is so much a part of our natures that we will nearly always do it in exactly the right place to give the right emphasis to the meaning of our words. The thought, by nature, goes together with the articulation and breath emphasis in forming sentences and phrases.

The interesting thing is that it does not matter what language we speak, or even whether we are speaking a foreign language we are just learning, there will always be a logic to the way we breathe and articulate which is related to, and enhances, the meaning of the words we are speaking: it seems almost impossible for us to deform the shape and timing under normal circumstances. But in instrumental playing we will not go with that logic enough. When we play the cello we get so self-conscious about the *craft* that we become unnatural. And the more self-conscious we become, the more unnatural and distorted our articulations, our sense of timing, our 'breathing' with the bow will be. We run phrases together like a fishing line running out without stop and forget to let the same natural logic and sense of timing that pervades our speech pervade our playing.

One can hardly over-stress the importance of 'breathing' in playing, and the importance for cellists to learn to 'breathe' with the bow: to pause and retake the bow again, to space between notes and between phrases in the same instinctive way they breathe and articulate in speech. All cellists need to learn to develop playing techniques which are the equivalent of the lips articulating, the lungs taking in air.

The means to articulation

One cannot talk about bowing articulations without talking about the means for achieving those articulations. The ability of the right hand to create the articulations – and the sense of tension, release and thrust, we need in playing – is determined by the use of the first finger as it sits on the stick. This is the perfect 'articulator' and it will determine the degree of contact at that point where the bow meets the string – the point of fusion between the downward pressure and the horizontal movement. The other fingers are essential in varying degrees, but they play their part always in relation to the leadership of the first finger.

To demonstrate this for yourself, try playing sometime with only your first finger on the stick and see how much sustaining power you can develop with that single finger alone. (In doing this exercise, if you begin at the frog, you will need to launch the bow with a normal grip and then release the fingers once the bow is in motion. See the illustrations on page 158.) Then you can relate the need for the other fingers according to the role that each one has to play in fulfilling the whole picture. By playing detached bows in the upper half of the bow, you will have the clearest idea of the use of the first finger as the principal shaping force in the right hand. From there you can begin to bow gradually closer and closer to the frog and observe how the other fingers begin to establish the complete hold as they are called upon to counterbalance the weight of the stick.

The experiment should strengthen the realization and understanding that the first finger against the stick provides the greatest means of transferring power from the arm into the stick (and hence to the hair and string). I stress this because I am aware that many people, when they want to play loudly, feel they need to grip the bow tightly with all four fingers. Yet the truth is that the biggest sound you will ever make on the cello comes from leading with the first finger and allowing the other fingers their roles relative to that. Nothing blocks sound like four stiffened fingers on the bow stick.

When you develop the sensation of contact via the first finger, you will begin to feel that the bow seems to sit in a groove in the string when you are playing. This groove becomes almost a physical sensation you can feel in your hand, the way you can 'feel' the grip of the tyres on the road when you are driving (and, conversely, the way you know when the tyres have lost their grip and are starting to skid). The feeling for the 'grooves' in the string is not only a sensation in the hand, but a sensation in the ear as well. The ear has its equivalent 'feel' for when the bow is gripping the string and travelling smoothly in the 'groove', and when it has lost its grip and is starting to skid.

When I speak of a 'groove', however, the last thing I want to imply is that there is but *one* single furrow or slot on the strings between the fingerboard and the bridge where the bow should always sit; there are, in fact, an infinite number of 'grooves' in the space allotted to the bow on the strings, and I will come to them in a minute; but one must first develop a feeling for the contact of the hair on the string, whatever groove one is playing in.

Choosing textures and colours

Within the boundaries of that small space on the strings between (roughly) the fingerboard and the bridge there dwells the richest variety of colours, textures and dynamics imaginable. There lies everything: the tenderness, the hardness, the soft-edged sounds, the brittleness. It is up to us to understand them, and know how to find them and how to use them. It is all there in that tiny space. Yet it is amazing how people will play through every dynamic and every emotion with their bow sitting in the same narrow area, never thinking to venture either upwards or downwards to explore the different edges their sound might have, the different tensions that are there for the taking.

Sound creation on the cello is not just a matter of playing more loudly or softly; it is necessary to use a whole range of varying qualities, voice modulations and articulations. Many cellists appear to be unconscious of the discrepancy between the colours and textures in a piece of music and the means to produce those colours and textures. They limit their physical concept to the narrow confines of a single 'voice' and modulation: it is like going through life experiencing the full range of emotions, from whispering sweet nothings to raging tempers, and saying everything in the same voice colour. Yet there is a wide range of sound qualities and textures available to use on our cellos, and as musicians we have an obligation to use all of them as required by the temper of the music. We must learn the laws of the nature of sound and how these relate to where our bow lives in the string, and it must become our absolute instinct to play in the appropriate place on the string for what we are trying to say.

Seven

The Limitation of Technique through the Comfort of Habit

The sensation of comfort should not blind one to musical fact.

Fingerings and bowings either fit the musicality of a phrase or do not, and we must never let the comfort of our well-worn paths so benumb our responses to the ear and the musical imagination that we cease to exercise musical judgement over what we play.

I often find that when I stop a student because he has played something I consider to be musically wrong and ask him why he used that particular fingering or bowing (the culprit of the musical distortion, in my opinion), the answer comes back, 'Well, I find it comfortable.' When I say, 'I'm not interested in your comfort or discomfort in this passage', it is not because I am not concerned about his comfort in the truest sense of the word, but because the student usually has so narrowed the area of what he calls 'comfortable', through one habitual way of playing something, that he has created a situation for himself where his very sense of comfort or discomfort, mental or physical, may be false. And he indulges his sense of 'comfort' often at the expense of the music.

It is amazing how 'comfortable' people can become in a physical action which is basically *un*comfortable, just because they have done it so long, to the exclusion of any other action. It is easy to tread the path of a single bowing or fingering so deep that all other possibilities seem like breaking new territory and therefore feel less comfortable. But if we give other possibilities a chance, and develop them equally, then we may discover that our old pet fingering or bowing turns out to be the least comfortable in the end. There are, in fact, many more paths in which one can be comfortable than most people allow themselves to have.

There is nothing wrong with habit, I might add, but one must have a large repertoire of habits. If one's sensation of comfort is based on narrow habit alone, then it is bound to be untrustworthy. Every cellist should train himself to be at home with several fingerings in a passage. By doing so he will build for himself a gigantic interlocking network where the paths of habit are not just single isolated tracks, but work more like a huge railway junction with the tracks crossing over one another and joining with one another to open up countless new possibilities of direction. (When the cellist has learned to become comfortable in that kind of complex situation, incidentally, he will find that he has at the same time developed a tremendous discernment, which will aid him in his musical decisions.)

Of course there will always be times when the physical is asked to do something which is against its nature because the ear demands it for musical reasons. These occasions present real problems, which have to be coped with on their own terms. But why add to that kind of real problem by bringing to one's playing an additional range of unnecessary discomfort created only through lack of stretching oneself out physically and mentally? Why narrow what in the first place needs to be widened? Why not open up as many paths as possible?

Comfort and the ear

Comfort for the sake of comfort (whether out of habit or for other reasons) not only places limitations on our technical growth but is one of the greatest enemies of the ear, and so of our musical judgement and discrimination.

How can we hope to determine the musical values of a passage if we become so tied to a single way of playing it that the ear is no longer given the chance to discriminate and guide, if we have become so satisfied in the comfort of a well-worn path that we successfully blot out of our consciousness all the imperfections and inadequacies the ear should be receiving and telling us about?

Purity of vision and the birth of concept

It is all too easy to start out being so 'busy' with the cello – deciding to take this fingering or that bowing before we have given any thought to what the fingering or bowing will do to the shape of the music – that we do not even notice when we have distorted a shape. But the fact is that any time we allow ourselves to begin by grappling with the one-sided issue of 'cello playing', we shall run the risk of pushing and pulling the music into any shape that is physically convenient. This, more than anything, will destroy our ability to develop a pure concept of the music's form and content.

Whenever we choose a fingering or a bowing, it should be because of its *musical* values. It is always the mood, the line, the emotion of the music that should dictate our choice of fingerings and bowings. If we want to discover and understand the inner nature of the shape of a piece of music, we have to approach it with a certain purity of mind, a mind uncluttered by personal whims or habits on the cello – a mind that is able to free itself from our own selves and our instrument and think purely as a creative entity. Personal whim, and a tendency to be influenced by physical convenience, which is not founded upon an understanding of the architecture of the music can only lead to musical chaos.

Eight
Bowings and Musical Shape

Making up one's mind about bowings before one has given sufficient thought to the shape of the musical phrase or structure is unlikely to produce something musically satisfying and valid. Whether this happens for the sake of physical convenience or out of habit, or according to convention, or because one has blindly accepted the bowings some editor put there without bothering to form one's own opinion, the fact remains that the cellist has lost sight of the real determining factor in his choice of bowings. Ultimately only the shape of the musical phrase, and of the units within the phrase, can determine the choice of bowings – it is misguided to think that they can be worked out apart from an understanding of this shape.

The shape of the line or phrase is always there to be seen by the naked eye or, if you prefer, to be heard by the naked ear. But, because we have to change bows, it is easy for string players to lose their feel for the line. Yet these very bow changes are crucial to the shaping of any line. If our bow change is misplaced by just one note, we shall have destroyed the very thing a right bowing could have achieved.

The root of the problem of bowings lies in habits that go back to a cellist's earliest training. String players begin by learning to group notes within the stroke of the bow – scales with two, three, four notes to the bow and, later, uneven groupings. Then they do little studies with the bowings laid out to utilize these groupings and give them practice using them in a larger context. (It is hard to imagine how else one could begin to master the necessary division of the bow). But when these arbitrary groupings, and the physical and mental habits thus engendered, get carried into later playing, the tendency to arrange bowings according to physical and mental habit often imposes a limitation upon a musical line, which may require a completely different shape, a shape which would be readily apparent if we could somehow learn to approach it with an innocent mind – a mind and body not blinkered by habit or a narrow sense of 'comfort' engendered by that habit.

Using bowings to shape the musical line

Through choice of bowings, we can either create or destroy the musical structure of a piece of music. Take as an example this passage from the Prelude of Bach's Suite in D minor for solo cello:

The illustration, here in Anna Magdalena Bach's hand, of bars 23–5, gives almost no bowings. It was perhaps never intended that it should be played with separate bows, but by starting out with the open mind that separate bows not only allow but foster, it is usually easier to discover the true shape of the line. In this particular passage, by playing with separate bows, one comes to understand that the upward line of the first seven notes of the second bar is a unit which is set off from the remaining five notes in the bar. Once this shape is understood, one can then choose to manifest it within the context of the separate bows, or one can organize the seven notes into a single bow (which I prefer) to set them off from the following downward unit. There is nearly always more than one bowing which will give a phrase its shape, but *it is always the shape of the line that must determine the bowing.*

Modern editing

One of the greatest problems (and tragedies) of our age is that the shape of a musical line is often forced into a false mould of arbitrary bowings by modern editing. Probably every cellist has seen editions of the passage just quoted bowed in even groups of four:

Yet musically it makes no more sense to group these notes in this way than it does verbally to group the letters in this sentence in even groups of four (thel ette rsin this sent ence inev engr oups offo ur)! In music, as with the written word, this type of arbitrary grouping makes it very difficult for the player to see beyond the distorted façade created by arbitrary bowings and discern the true line hidden beneath. The all-important issue in translating the shape of a line of music is the choice of a bowing that will give that shape its existence. Our choice of bowings must therefore always begin with and grow out of a conscious attempt to perceive that shape. Ingrained bowing habits are never a valid starting point.

The Prelude to the C major suite by Bach illustrates in a different way just how crucial bowings are in creating the sense of the line. In this passage (bars 7–13) there is a 'hidden' voice which forms the superstructure of the passage, and the cellist will need to select his bowings in a way that will bring out that voice and separate it from the rest of the line. (The notes of the 'hidden' tune are indicated by *x*.)

The Cello

Because the Prelude to this Suite offers so many excellent examples of how shape can be created (or destroyed) by the cellist's choice of bowings, I would like to include the full musical text here, on pages 66–9, with bowings and markings to show the shape of the lines as I see them, in order to give cellists a point of departure for further exploration in this direction on their own.

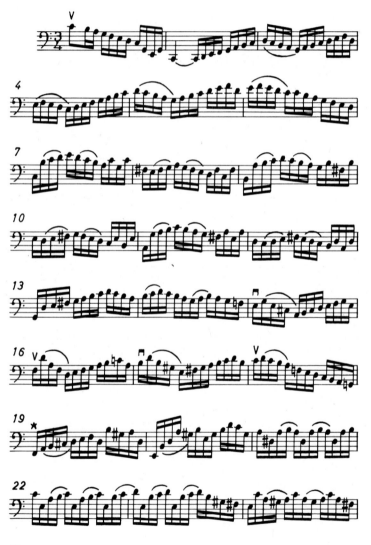

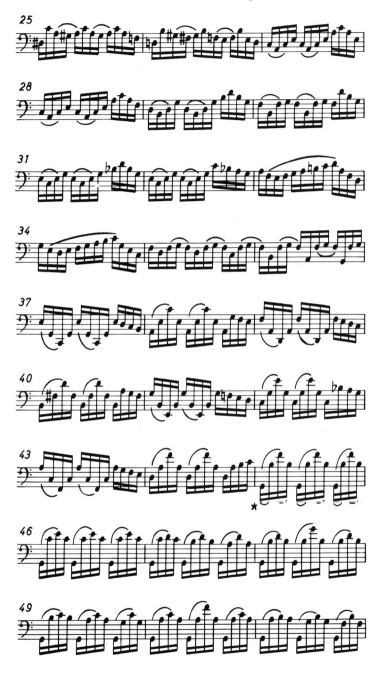

Once we understand the shape of a phrase, then *it* will guide us to the bowings needed to give it its existence; in the end it is not 'bowings' in the abstract sense we are after, but ways of using our bow to fulfil the *inherent* shape of a musical line. As I have already pointed out, there is often more than one bowing that can do this in a particular passage: different bowings, provided they are based on the same underlying logic, will only be different ways of serving the same end. Without an understanding of the musical shape, however, we cannot even start to look for bowings – we are flying blind. We must seek an understanding of the musical shape first, and then let *it* sow the seeds that will later blossom into perhaps several bowing possibilities.

Nine
The Architecture of Music

Form should be your religion in art, and purity of vision your strongest guide.

The most important thing in any work of art is form. The absence of form is chaos. The greatest crime is distortion of form, and the greatest virtue is the understanding and creation of the beauty of a shape, a curve, the logic of an architectural line in music. The great masterpieces of our repertoire should be absolutely shattering; but when they are played without a sense of form, without an understanding of the architecture that is the very core of their being, they are reduced to nonsense.

From the time of the Greeks and Romans man has maintained that harmony in architecture is as satisfying to the eye as harmony in music is to the ear, that the impact on the human heart is the same whether the original stimulus is visual or aural. The truth of this is obvious. What the eye conveys to the mind and heart when one sees the perfection of beauty and logic in a Renaissance arch or colonnade is something more than the simple sensation of an optical image; it is something one can actually *feel* as well. What the eye is seeing has its counterpart in the human heart. In music we have the equivalent of this in the shape of a phrase, in the architecture of a movement, in the structure of the whole work. The importance of architecture, whether in visual or aural spheres, lies in the effect it has on the human heart.

One may choose to view 'architecture' in music as the external shape, or shell, into which the emotional content of the music fits and through which it derives its form; or one may view it as an internal superstructure, like the skeleton of the body, upon which the emotional shape of the music is moulded (both analogies will be used in the course of this chapter); but, however one chooses to view it, the cellist – every musician – should understand that it is the architecture of a piece of music which is one's light-giver. It, above all else, is what determines the shape and quality of all that one does on the cello – the colours one uses, the choice of textures, the dynamics, the rhythm, the rubato, and the bowings and fingerings.

Without an all-encompassing sense of the architecture of a piece of music (or even a single phrase or line), it becomes all too easy for musicians to lose their way in a self-created thicket of personal whims and technical accommodation. Virtually every concerto and most sonatas are full of passages which can tempt one to shift gears and lurch into each new bit as if it had no relationship to the surrounding musical terrain or to the structure as a whole. One has to resist this temptation to nibble at the little bits: however pretty one makes them, they are architecturally meaningless on their own. It is only when the bits are put in their proper position structurally, and the emotional shape of each little bit takes its place in relation to the overall concept, that they become something wonderful. Only through a thorough understanding of the architecture of the music, and the subsequent subjugation of one's physical and mental conveniences to the overriding musical consideration of the architecture, can one fit all the smaller units into a meaningful whole.

Architectural form and emotional content

When one talks about musical architecture, one is really talking about 'emotional shapes'. The emotional content of a piece of music is so much a part of its architectural form that we cannot separate the one from the other. Because of this, our most important consideration when

71

we approach a piece of music (and however many times throughout our lives we approach the same piece of music) should be a passionate search for the form of the work and the recreation of that form in sound.

'Form' in the fullest sense of the word embraces not only the external structure of a piece of music – *sonata form* or *rondo form*, say – but all the many qualities of sound that live within the shell of the outer structure and build it from within. Form is both the logic of design that precedes a work of art, and the filling out of that logic with all that it must contain in order to make it live and convey an emotional and aesthetic experience. Thus we cannot (or should not) develop our ideas of the emotional shape of a passage until we have understood the architecture that governs that shape. It is first and foremost the architecture of a work or phrase that is going to determine the direction of the musical emotion and the musical spontaneity, and which imposes upon the player the technical command needed to achieve its fulfilment.

Architecture and interpretation

The problem confronting the performer in matters concerning architecture is quite a different one from that confronting the composer. A fine composer, by writing down something he feels, creates the form of the music simultaneously with the emotional content that fills it out. The two are inseparable from the moment of conception within his mind. This is not to say that the composer does not have his agonizing moments of trial and error; he, too, is reaching out for something. But at every point along his path to their creation, the two things, form and content, exist as two aspects of a single entity. The performer, however, when he begins to look at a piece of music, must of necessity start from outside the circle of creation and then work his way into the circle in order to discover the unity that was complete in the composer's mind from the very beginning. He has to probe beneath the surface and discover the structure hidden within, and the emotion that that structure generates. (There are rare situations, of course; where the performer works closely with the composer on a particular composition and thereby becomes privy to the process of creation, at least to a certain degree – but this is the exception rather than the rule.)

The act of discovery on the part of the performer needs a purity of integrity – and tremendous respect for even the minutest details of the composer's instructions, for they are his only means of transmitting his message on paper. Therefore, we must never start out by putting our own personality in between. The music is not there to become a plaything for our whims. If we depart from what the composer has given us, then we have altered his original intent.

Let me give just one example of this kind of tampering with the composer's intent: in the passage quoted below one can imagine that Brahms was looking for a sound effect similar to that of the gypsy cymbalon which he loved from Hungarian folk music:

Brahms: Sonata in F, first mov't, bars 60–61

But how frequently one hears it rearranged as double stops:

either because the performer has missed the point of what Brahms was after, or because he finds it physically more convenient to play double stops. Whatever the reason, the result is a complete distortion of the composer's intention as expressed in the notation (we have to assume that if Brahms had intended double stops, he knew well enough how to write them). Every work must be approached in a pure and unadulterated way if one is to arrive at fresh conclusions, determined by the nature of that particular composition and untainted by conventional interpretations, clichés and personal whim.

Playing by hearsay

There is so much 'playing by hearsay' these days that a great masterpiece often ends up like a 'rumour' which is passed so much by word of mouth that it eventually loses all relation to the original truth. Sadly, in the world of performance, there is often such an unquestioned acceptance of these 'hearsay' distortions that players go on repeating every mannerism, every cliché, without ever noticing that the composer never put it there.

Think of the ending of the Minuet in the second movement of the Brahms E minor Sonata:

It has become tradition to play it with spread chords and a ritard (because that is the most obvious way of ending something). But Brahms did not write a ritard, or spread chords; and if we play it that way, only because we have so often heard it that way, then we have missed its emotional subtlety. If, on the other hand, we follow Brahms's directions more closely, we might even find ourselves discovering a greater beauty in it than we had imagined, a simplicity reminiscent of certain endings in Mendelssohn's music. It is in relation to the architectural and emotional demands of the music, not by 'hearsay', that our musical ideas have to be developed. Not only will it give us a fresher approach, but it will develop in us a continual flow of related imagination as a way of musical life.

What is written down in black and white can have many lives, and we must never fear that we will lose our individuality when we harness our minds and spirits to the intent of the music. There are many ways of saying something which has been created by someone else without distorting its emotional intent or its architecture. In the end one discovers that it is not a question of subjugating one's personality to that of the composer, but rather of using one's insights in the right sort of way *vis-à-vis* the music. It is an investigation, a test, and a climbing point, too, for our own person, and it is only when we start this way that we can spread our wings with the music.

Playing cadenzas

A cellist's understanding of the architecture of the whole becomes particularly crucial when, in a concerto, he feels that a cadenza is appropriate. I think that the idea of 'cadenza' shocks people into thinking 'technical feat', and they approach cadenzas thinking, 'Now I am supposed to show what I can do on the cello.'

In reality, the cadenza should be a bridge, a comment on a movement that brings one back to the tutti, a little reminiscence touching upon snatches of melody from the movement. Yet one sees in many cellists a greedy ambition to make a whole new work of the cadenza. They take all the showier passages from the movement and string them together (minus the musical cohesion put there originally by the composer), add to them a lot of common-place cellistic clichés designed to dazzle, and end up with something which is nearly as long as the movement but is lacking in cohesion and in any sense of proportion to the movement as a whole.

One would think that if a cellist has not been able to create an impact with the showier passages when they were set in a context of some musical merit, then there is not much value in having a second shot at them when they are all strung together without the musical binding of the composer. Certainly it is difficult to understand why anyone would want to go into such lower worlds of show-off technique when one has just been indulging in the musical experience of a great piece of music (already demanding the greatest command of technique).

There are, it goes without saying, many cadenzas which one can rightfully admire, but for some reason concerto performance by cellists seems so bereft of musically meaningful cadenzas and so rife with showy passage work which displays a completely wrong understanding of what a cadenza ought to be, that one longs for a sense of balance. A cadenza must never lose sight of its purpose in relation to the whole of the movement and lead the listener too far away from the greater musical experiences provided by the composer.

Tartini, in his *Traité des Agréments* (*c.* 1746) gives several sketches for possible eighteenth-century cadenzas, outlining the architectural skeleton and then indicating many different kinds of figuration one could use to link the main harmonic points. Here is but one illustration:

In the twentieth century Mátyás Seiber gives a similar outline for a cadenza in his violin sonata, again leaving it to the performer to fill in the material between the main points. Cellists can use these ideas and suggestions to build upon when they are formulating their own ideas about cadenzas.

In any case, one would like to encourage cellists to think a little more about cadenzas – and one would hope that they would in time come to lose this compulsion (or sense of obligation) to put overblown cadenzas into an otherwise beautifully structured piece of music. I know it is the fashion to play this kind of cadenza, but still a cadenza must relate, it must have discretion and not become a work on its own. One would like to see cellists have the courage to begin to improvise little cadenzas for themselves: to sketch something short and know how to make it weave in and out of the main fabric of the movement. It may comprise one's personal thoughts on a movement, but it should always be kept in proportion to the musical whole.

Ten
The Ingredients of Architecture

Architecture in music depends upon the form of the individual parts, and embraces the many worlds of colour, texture, dynamics, rhythm and rubato. It is through the subtle combination of all these ingredients that the musical line is given its shape, the musical architecture its existence.

I: Colour and texture

It is an unnecessary restriction of our instrument's potential if we let the fact that the cello is but a single instrument trap us into treating it as 'one sound'. The cello has the capacity for such a vast range of sound qualities, if we use it rightly, that the limitations can only be ones of our own making. It is our imagination, not the instrument, which is limited.

Many cello students have allowed their imagination for colour and texture variety to atrophy because they have developed the physical habit of producing only one sound on the cello. They play different tempi, they play loud, they play soft, and it all comes down to the same thing because they lay over all the vast and differing ranges of compositions, styles and sentiments the single emotional blanket of one sound – only the notes are different. In doing so they unwittingly destroy their own attempts to realize the intent and emotional impact of a work, and at the same time starve their technical development (which would flourish if it were but allowed to function on a wider and more subtle plane).

Why should we wrap everything in the single emotional blanket of one sound? Music cannot all be the same, and so the sounds we use to create it cannot all be the same. One would hope rather that the immense variety of sound qualities demanded by our repertoire, even within the works of one composer or any single work, would inspire cellists to develop a greater sensitivity to the sound and shading of every single note. Not to be able to distinguish between the musical language of composers as diverse as, say, Bach, Beethoven and Debussy, and to create in one's playing the vastly different worlds of colours and textures which are a part of the language and the very temperament of these composers, is to me an intolerable impoverishment of our art and our craft.

Musical shape through string colour

The creation and communication of musical architecture is dependent in large part upon the performer's choice of colour and texture and the way he uses them to help shape the line. String players who are concerned about widening their scope for potential colour and texture portrayal, particularly as these relate to musical shape and architecture, will find it essential to investigate the ways in which these qualities are modified by their choice of one string over another, and through the way sound can be developed on one string as opposed to another.

We talked earlier on about the endless variety of textures available to us through the sensitive and imaginative use of bow/string contact (i.e., where, in the area between the bridge and fingerboard, one chooses to place the bow on the string); when these possibilities are combined with the additional colour and texture potential available to us through the different qualities of the four strings, we find ourselves in possession of an almost unlimited range of expressive possibilities. But only when we have learned to explore the colour and texture potentialities of each string, and to combine them judiciously, will we be in a position to use them in a way that will help fulfil the musical shape of a line.

What, for instance, do we look for in a group of rising notes? Is it enough to see each note as being simply higher than the preceding note, or is there a life inside that 'higherness' which suggests a completely different feel or direction to the line, a different meaning to the phrase? There is an enormous difference in the shape of a line when we take a group of notes up on the same string and when we cross strings to play those same notes. Each choice embraces a completely different world of string colour and texture, and we have to be conscious of what these different choices of colour can imply, and to recognize the importance of the choice we make relative to our overall concept of the passage or phrase. Above all we have to realize that everything we play implies a choice; and it is important that that choice is a conscious one and not just a blind acceptance of the first colour that comes to hand.

Learning to use our sound potential in this way demands something far beyond a simple recognition of the basic colour of each string – treating each string as a primary colour and then contrasting it with the single primary colour of another string. It demands an ability to discover and command the many hues of colour that exist within each string, and the knowledge of how they relate to the many other hues inherent in the other strings. How we combine these determines how we shape the music.

Through our use of colour and texture, for instance, a passage can be made to open out and bloom, or it can be made to stay inside itself and grow darker and more enclosed. It should fascinate us to discover how easily we can create illusions of colour and texture, of light and shadow, of various degrees of tension and pull, of space opening up or compacting, through the way we choose our string colours and textures. More important, however, this kind of investigation will enable our playing to bring to light the inner nature of the music's lyrical and dramatic qualities and allow them to make their fullest impact.

When exploited to its fullest, the range for string colour and texture is almost endless – especially on the cello, where the wider range of string textures, from the relatively relaxed sound of the open C string to the tautness and brightness of the higher reaches of the A string, allows the fullest compass for variety in colour and texture. Such an array of colour possibilities demands of us all a high degree of discernment and a dedication to exploration and discovery.

Fingering choices and colour

String colour and texture is where the question of fingering really starts, and why it is so important. It is often easier and safer to choose the more conventional fingering, the more pedagogical way, but this leaves us with much less capacity for the subtle shading that the music often needs. We need instead to become more courageous and imaginative in exploring fingering possibilities and discovering how these relate to colours and textures. But to do this we must shake off the habit of staying within the basic pathways we were first taught, for it is habit which limits the fantasy and stultifies the imagination. We cannot approach fingerings, and the colours and textures they engender, with a one-track mind. Nor can we allow ourselves to be so in love with our own fingering clichés that we lose our capacity for exploring. A narrow concept of fingerings only blinkers us to all the endless possibilities there are, and to the obligation we have to develop our imagination and fantasy to the fullest.

Almost any group of notes can be played in a different way – on another string, or with a different combination of strings, or on the same strings but changing over in another place. Cellists must consider these other possibilities and try them; they must want to explore, and say, 'Let me have a shot at another fingering, another choice of strings, and see what that tells me.' It could even tell them what was right about their original choice. And even if one is wrong in what one tries, it could still open new doors and lead on to something else more fruitful.

'Voice inflections' through colour and texture

In speech, the words in a phrase and the phrases in a sentence have different sounds according to their context and the emotion that stands behind them. Take any word you commonly use and you will find that as it reoccurs in your speech you will instinctively give it different inflections according to its role.

When we go to the theatre, we certainly expect the actors to convey the meaning and sentiment of the words they speak through voice modulations which involve colour and texture – if they did not, then simply staying home and reading the script would be just as satisfying. But if we take this for granted with actors, should not we musicians have an equivalent sensitivity in the production of our sounds? Should not the actor's voice inflections have their counterpart in music? Surely it is just as important for musicians to sense how colours and textures fit within the meaning of a musical sentence and how they determine the relation of that sentence to the larger aspects of a work. We cannot limit every 'word' in a musical sentence to the same sentiment – the same type of love, intensity, colour, sensuousness, or what-have-you; musical sentences have the same great potential for emotional expression as an actor's lines (more, we would often like to think) and they have the same great need for modification of sound colours and textures to convey that expression.

Portrayal and characterization

The way we use words in a sentence is but a part of the larger world of *characterization*. In portraying a character through the lines he speaks, an actor's first task is to imagine the nature of that character and then to develop the voice inflections and other colorations of speech that will best portray its nature.

Musical performance, too, demands *portrayal* and *characterization*, but the role of the musician is often more complicated because the nature of most of our music is such that we have to encompass within our one being many different characters. It makes no more sense for a cellist to speak in one 'voice' all the time, to have everything sound as if it were coming out of one mouth, than it would for an actor who was taking the part of many characters in a play to speak all the various lines in a single, undifferentiated voice (however rich and sonorous). In any great work in our repertoire there are many different lines requiring different 'characters' to speak them, and it is essential that cellists should both recognize them and know how to let each speak with its own voice.

Orchestration

In purely musical terms one may prefer to think of this kind of voice differentiation as *orchestration*. In symphonic writing a score comes into existence because a composer uses different instruments, and groups of instruments, to convey the sound of different colours and textures – to portray different 'characters' as it were. When the number of instruments in a composition is reduced to a chamber ensemble, quartet, duo or even solo sonata, it does not implicitly follow that the range of colours and textures will be reduced proportionately. We all know that a symphony orchestra is capable of a vast range of colours; but a string quartet does not sound incomplete or limited because there are only four instruments – their completeness rests upon a more highly developed use of colour and texture.

The stature and emotional range of a composition should not be smaller just because it is written for a smaller ensemble, or even for a solo instrument; each has within its own framework an equivalent range of musical personalities. Numbers have nothing to do with it. Who would contend that Leonardo da Vinci's *Mona Lisa* has less emotional vitality than Botticelli's *La Primavera* just because it has fewer figures in it? Or that the Kodály Solo

Sonata makes less of an emotional impact than one of his orchestral works? The smaller the ensemble, the more important it becomes for each player to be able to portray an even wider range of colour and characterization.

The concept of colour over the centuries

String music of earlier centuries implies a broader concept of the subtle use of colour and texture quite beyond the practice of the average cellist today. It seems ironic that our concepts of sound textures and colour range should have become so narrowed in the twentieth century. One would have expected just the opposite – that our vantage point would enable us to incorporate the wonderful colours, the infinite degrees of shading, the subtleties of colour and texture nuance of earlier centuries into our playing and use them to enhance the works of every period.

It is an enormous loss if we throw away the immense variety of the past just because we have developed a handful of new sounds. We *need* these earlier sounds even in our modern music. Listen to some of the Shostakovich quartets: the incredibly cool colours they want in places, the tremendous variation of vibrato needed to create these colours. Look at the whole landscapes of colour and texture contrast in the Bartók quartets or in the Kodály or Debussy sonatas. How can we fulfil the needs of this music if we allow ourselves to be cut off from the subtleties of colour and texture of earlier epochs and confine ourselves to the 'big, warm' sound people seem to prize today? Why should we shut doors behind us as we progress on our journey into new realms of sound and expression? All life is a continuum, and all music and musical performance should be based on a sense of continuity which enlarges upon the past to enrich the present.

The composer's world of colour

We must never allow ourselves to lose sight of the colours and textures in sound that were a part of each composer's world. It is nearly impossible for any composer to avoid being steeped in the sound concepts which prevail throughout his lifetime, and each composition he writes must reflect to some degree the sound world into which the piece was born; but it is our role as performers to live in *all* the worlds of sound that are part of our repertoire. How can we hope to penetrate to the depths of the music of any composer – be it Bach, Brahms or Bartók – if we allow ourselves to become so limited in our concepts of sound that we cannot even imagine the colours and textures that were a part of that composer's world, and if we do not command the rich palette of colours out of which his music grew? By attempting to approach the music of people like Beethoven from twentieth-century sound concepts *backwards*, instead of eighteenth-century concepts *forwards*, we only force the music into a mould it was never meant to fit.

Apart from compelling stylistic reasons, there looms an even bigger question: why should we *want* to confine ourselves to our present-day island of time when we could be linking up to a continuous archipelago of sound concepts and possibilities stretching back over centuries of string playing? Why not explore all the wonderful qualities of sound which earlier periods of music have given us – ranges of colour and texture, of dynamic, of bow articulations and vibrato variations which can lead us to wider horizons in the music of any period? We should want to encompass all this in our playing and make it a part of our world.

II: Dynamics in context

Dynamics are too often taken as an absolute, a measurable loudness, yet often our choice of colour and texture is more important in creating the sensation of a dynamic than is sheer decibel level. One texture can give greater clarity at a given dynamic, while another will impart a haziness to the sound; a bright colour can cause a dynamic

The Cello

to stand out from the surrounding countryside, while a darker colour will give the illusion that the dynamic is withdrawing. Thus the question of dynamics is never a matter of volume alone; it is how colour, texture and tension are used within a given volume to determine the outcome on a musical level. In musical performance we deal with the sensation of dynamics; it is the *illusion* we are after, because in music the illusion is the reality.

Variety within dynamics

The important thing is to allow our concept of dynamics to have a great variety within any single dynamic. Dynamics exist in unending variation. How many hearts are there in 'loud' or 'soft'? In the Franck Sonata the big, expansive *forte* as one comes to the climax in the first movement is quite a different sound from the hard, terse *forte* one needs to open the second movement. And, in the Dvořák Concerto, passages with the same dynamic markings can create completely different sensations of dynamic and mood. Compare the two passages given below:

pp più tranquillo

First mov't., bars 136–8

pp molto espress. e sostenuto

Ibid. bars 122–6

In the Haydn C major Concerto a virile *forte* (A) is set against a more gentle and lyrical *forte* (B) within the same passage:

First mov't., bars 67–9

Later in the same movement a *forte* of a tutti character (A) is set against a *forte* of a solo character (B):

Ibid., bars 110–12

Within the single dynamic marking of *forte* we can have a sound which is fat and heavy, or brittle and hard, or warm, or sensuous, or brutal, or severe, or pure, or 'solo' or 'tutti' – the possibilities are really as endless as the emotional qualities of music.

Dynamics can even be used imaginatively to suggest a kind of 'orchestration'. We all know, for instance, that the *forte* of a trombone is different from the *forte* of a flute, and as you 'orchestrate' in your mind when you are playing, you will often want to use colours and textures to suggest a particular instrument at a given dynamic and thereby enhance the sensation of that dynamic in that particular musical situation.

Thus within any dynamic we have to be aware of the kind of sound that is suggested by the musical context. It is never merely a matter of *forte* or *piano* but much more a question of, 'What kind of *forte*?' or 'What kind of *piano*?' When we see a dynamic marking, we have to think colours, think textures, think orchestration and characterization – they will suggest the nature of the dynamic. Each passage within a given dynamic has to have its own heart; and if we fix a dynamic according to an imaginary absolute, it is almost certainly going to be out of step with the character of the music.

Composers and dynamics

Dynamic markings can only take on meaning when they are understood within the context of the emotion of the music and the characteristic language of the composer who put them there. What any composer intends by a dynamic marking is dependent in part upon his own temperament and nature and in part upon the historical period in which he lived. In order to play the music of any composer we have to be able to fit ourselves, our own mentality, into his world. The nature of a *forte* in Bach is not the same as a *forte* in Brahms; even signs like accents and *sforzandi* take on different meanings from one composer to another. Schubert, for instance, uses accents to indicate a gentle stress, while another composer, to get over the same degree of stress, might put a line over the note instead of an accent. Compare these passages from Schubert's *Arpeggione* Sonata and the cello sonata by Rachmaninov:

Schubert: Sonata in A; third mov't., bars 1–8

Rachmaninov: Sonata in G; fourth mov't., bars 1–7

Schumann treats accent marks in a way similar to Schubert, and when he wants a real accent he puts a *sfz* – which is something quite different from a *sfz* in Beethoven!

Dynamic contrasts

Just as a given *dynamic* is something more subtle than measurable loudness, a change in dynamic is something much more subtle than a shift from one measurable loudness to another. A dynamic change might embrace a different nature, a different sort of voice or a contrast of moods or tonal qualities. Whether the change is abrupt or whether it happens gradually (via a *crescendo* or *diminuendo*), the success of the emotional impact of the change will depend mainly upon the qualities that one puts inside the successive dynamics. We have already seen how many ingredients go into the creation of a dynamic. But a sudden shift of dynamics, or the gradual evolving of one dynamic into another, demands the use of these ingredients to create not only the sensation of dynamic change but often to create as well the feeling of a change of heart or voice.

The possibilities for variation within a *crescendo* for instance are endless; it all depends on how we use any number of other factors within the process of 'growing louder' in sound. A friendly, lyrical *crescendo*, for instance, might retain the same character as it gets louder. Or in a different musical setting it might get tighter and tighter and grow 'red in the face' as it gets louder. Or a passage might begin already 'red in the face' and bloom into a more relaxed and open-hearted sound as it grows.

A *diminuendo* in a passage that is already tight and tense might need to keep those qualities as the sound diminishes, letting the sound remain tight and tense as it grows smaller. But another kind of music might suggest the sort of *diminuendo* where everything is diminishing and unwinding; where the inner core of the sound loosens in a way that provides a perfect counterpart to the external diminishment of the sound, and the dynamic becomes a melting point, a point of unwinding. In this kind of musical situation it is not just a question of the measurement of the sound going down, but of the heart growing quieter as well. Change in volume is only a minute part of the wider world of dynamic change.

Transcending dynamics

Confusion of 'volume' with 'dynamics' is often the cause of musicians straining for sound and overplaying. Ironically, the more greedy for power one lets oneself become, the more insatiable the appetite – and the more one is tempted to use power indiscriminately (as, for instance, in many performances one hears of the Bach Suites, where the sound is used often to a maximum level).

We cellists, in particular, tend to get greedy about sound. If someone were to discover a way to make the cello sound twice as loud as it does, I am sure there are many of us who would want to play to that limit. Like greedy children, the more we get, the more we want; and eventually everything becomes so distorted that we lose not only all sense of proportion, but also all sense of what we were trying to do in the first place. Greed is not necessarily a bad thing, but why should our greed be all so one-sided? Why can't we get equally greedy for other more subtle qualities?

The desire to play to full power all the time seems to be fed in part by an inferiority complex many cellists have over the relatively small sound of the cello, and in part by the sheer physical sensation of the feel of power. Following these false paths, we are often led to indulge in brute force to the exclusion of *emotional* power. No matter how powerful a player you are, even if you are able to take the sound of the cello to its physical limits, you will never make the cello go into the volume of a trombone or cathedral organ. Once the cello has reached its physical limits, it is only something spiritual which can carry on beyond that, something which goes beyond the combined ingredients of one's physical self and the instrument. However immediately satisfying the sensation of sheer physical power may be, the truth is that in the end it is only emotional power which will be able to carry us beyond the purely physical limitations of the instrument. There will always come a point where the little cello has its end; then something else must carry us further – and it is not going to be the volume. Those of us who play an instrument such as the cello, with its admitted volume limitations, need to understand that we can still create the illusion of greater dynamic range through emotional projection.

What we are talking about here are realities which

transcend the black and white limits of physical fact: the reality that you can create a continuity of dramatic tension in a passage which will carry you beyond the point where your instrument can serve you. To do this you have to know where to stop the sheer brute force in order to create the greater dimensions of the spiritual power of the music. It is a bit like setting off a rocket: you leave one stage behind in order for the next to go on.

There are times, for instance, especially in the higher ranges, when greater emotional intensity and passion can only be achieved by relaxing and freeing the bow. If we do not cut loose from the earlier stage of the 'rocket' (which is sheer power), then the sound will begin to turn back on itself and start to bottle up. This, in turn, results in a fight for more and more sound – and as the projection of sound begins to disintegrate and crumble, the whole strength and drama of the music becomes side-tracked into a false world of frantic physical action which in the end only depletes the whole musical impact. It is amazingly easy to take that wrong path, and it needs tremendous discipline to go the other way when one is caught up in that kind of whirlpool.

The problem is that we are so used to matching our mental and emotional intensity with an equivalent physical intensity that it is difficult to realize that, after a certain point is reached, greater emotional intensity can only be achieved by backing off physically – while still retaining or even increasing the emotional projection. This is difficult, I know, because it requires one to do just the opposite of what one's natural instincts would be. But the fact remains that beyond a certain point greater intensity can only be achieved by realizing that the physical tension has come to the end of the line and that one has to let go of the physical so that a greater emotional projection can take over.

Decibel loudness has nothing to do with it. A person with a dramatic nature can convey more sense of dynamic scope on a tiny little fiddle than another person with a tiny spirit can on a nine-foot grand piano. It is not so much a question of making the sound bigger, as of making the sound *feel* bigger because you use a bigger spirit. Think of all those people in the eighteenth century who played on instruments which had much greater volume limitations than our modern cello, yet their range of emotional feeling was vast. They had an emotional stature that was in no way diminished by the fact that they could not take their instrument up to the decibel levels to which we are able to take ours today. This is the central truth of dynamics. If we understand this, then the nature of our instrument will never be an impediment to our expression of dynamics.

III: The role of vibrato

If vibrato is to have any meaning at all as an expressive element in music, it must be instinctively sensitive to what one is saying musically and emotionally. The unrelated and indiscriminate use of vibrato is, in my opinion, one of the greatest weaknesses in much cello playing. One goes to concerts and hears otherwise marvellous cellists playing a great variety of music, music which should have every mood and shading under the sun, all portrayed with a one-gear vibrato throughout. It is as if a colour-blind artist were slapping paint indiscriminately on the canvas with no understanding of how the different colours related to what he was trying to depict.

Musicians cannot allow themselves to become 'colour-blind' in the ear. At any level of command, we should develop commensurate ability and discipline in the left hand to shade our vibrato through all the unending degrees of quality, sound modulation and mood, from the purest thread of sound, with complete stillness in the left hand, right up through to the most dramatic and passionately expressive powers.

Vibrato in relation to the whole
Perhaps vibrato is viewed too narrowly because there has been too much emphasis placed upon it for its own sake

without any consideration of why, when and what for. Cellists in particular have tended to isolate it as a virtue in itself, forgetting that it becomes a virtue only when it is rightly related to the emotional sense and architecture of a passage and to the colours, textures, and dynamics that create that emotional sense and architecture.

If one says that a vibrato is 'better' because it is bigger, or because it is even, then that is not necessarily relating it to the sentiment of the music. If the music is, for instance, cooler, then one should say 'better' when the vibrato is cooler; it might be better because there is less of it, or because it is more thoughtful and not just going on its own sweet friendly way. All facets of sound production are so closely tied in with one another that they have to exist as one thing within the mind and within the whole musical being. Vibrato shades just as colours, textures, dynamics and intensities do, and the way we use our vibrato has to be a part of our total musical concept.

Vibrato's wide potential and its narrow use

It is amazing how quick we all are to appreciate the role of vibrato in creating expressive qualities in other areas of musical performance, and yet how consistently we turn a deaf ear to its unvaried use in string playing. Almost any sensitive string player who listens to a Byrd Mass sung by a fine men and boys' choir will be thrilled by the purity of sound and by the way the clear quality of that sound serves the spirit of the music. Similarly, if he hears the Verdi Requiem sung by great operatic singers, he will find that equally beautiful in a totally different way. But if one were to turn the two around and have the choir sing Verdi and the operatic singers sing Byrd, he would almost certainly be repelled by sound qualities which are disastrously misplaced. Yet this same person, when he is engaged in his own playing, often fails to recognize misplacement of sound qualities (especially as relates to vibrato), which are just as disastrous for the music he is playing.

Such misplacement of sound qualities has, sadly,

become so commonplace in string playing that even audiences have come to accept a perversion of sound, colour and style that would shock their sensibilities were they to hear it in any other medium. Time and again you hear people say of a cellist, 'Hasn't he got a lovely tone?', or a 'beautiful' tone, or a 'sweet' tone. Rarely does one hear the other expressive qualities, which are so linked with judicious variety in the use of vibrato, extolled. But what if the music is not 'sweet' or 'lovely'? How often, actually, does one see the word *dolce* (meaning 'sweetly') written into the music? And what does the cellist who habitually plays with a sweet, *dolce* sound then do when he actually encounters the word *dolce* in the score?

Surely it must be obvious that there cannot be sameness throughout a creative work of art. But one fears that even in many very fine players the ear somehow has not remained sensitive to this aspect of playing. So many have allowed themselves to overlook the simple fact that subtlety of colour creation in the left hand, and the fulfilment of dynamic nuance, require the sensitive use of vibrato.

The fallacy of the single vibrato
One suspects that cellists' blindness to the variety they could and should have in vibrato is due in large part to the way they regard the whole subject of vibrato. One often hears them talk about 'a' vibrato, or 'their' vibrato, or they discuss what 'type' of vibrato they prefer, as if they were discussing what style of suit they like best. One even hears of remarkably fine players going to this teacher or that to get this or that kind of vibrato. You would think that vibrato was something you bought in a shop, and that once you had decided upon the model you liked best you wore it for every occasion. Never mind the vast expressive range of music, just dress it all in the single suit of one vibrato!

The root of the problem lies in the fact I alluded to earlier that we have been educated to one 'noise', one sound on the cello. And in the pursuit of that one sound we have closed our minds and imaginations to myriad other possibilities. We have allowed the taste-buds of our musical palates when we get on the cello to become so used to a single sensation of one sound that we are shocked by a new or different sound and, reacting in terms of that shock, pronounce it 'bad' or ugly. But the only ugly sounds are those which are either badly produced or which, however well produced, do not fit the musical context.

Why should we have just one vibrato? A composer does not have just one mood. We should be happy to seize upon the wealth of expressive possibilities available to us through a highly developed use of unlimited shades of vibrato. The essence of musical taste and expression dictates that we use every degree, every shade of vibrato – and it demands of us the sensitivity and discipline to portray it.

Many young cellists, I fear, develop bad vibrato habits because they become so enamoured by the 'glamorous' sound which vibrato can simulate that they fail to develop the basic beauty of sound which only the right hand can create (or perhaps they have allowed the attitudes of other more advanced cellists to infect them with a false and limited concept of what 'beauty' in sound is). They then spend the rest of their lives trying to compensate for this deficiency by covering up their undeveloped basic sound with an ever thicker coating of vibrato. By misusing the basic facts of sound production and misunderstanding the relationship of the ingredients that go into it, they lose sight of the basic truth that there will never be great beauty of sound and expression in any sphere if there is not a basic beauty of sound production to begin with – and this starts not in the left hand but in the *right*. We must begin with the pure creation of sound in the right hand before we even start to attack the problem of vibrato in the left.

Bringing the hand under control
To develop sensitivity in vibrato, one must first bring the hand under control, recleanse it and train it away from its involuntary wobble. A perpetual-motion vibrato is, after

all, an acquired habit. We were none of us born with it, and we should be able to play with a completely pure, unadorned sound which is both beautiful and appropriate to certain sentiments in music.

Cellists who have developed bad vibrato habits must find a way to return to the 'innocent' hand they once had and retrain it in a way that will allow it to become responsive to the music. Starting from a perfectly still and uncontaminated (or uncontaminat*ing*) left hand, they should first see how pure and marvellous the sound from the right hand can be; and from that pure beginning, they can begin to develop the sound with the vibrato.

I find the most practical vehicle for bringing the hand under control and teaching it to become comfortable throughout all ranges of vibrato is the scale. Because of its simplified and familiar lay-out, the scale removes other concerns and distractions and allows one to concentrate on the purest creation of sound. It may seem a bit clinical to practise vibrato in this way, but it is often necessary to be clinical at first in order to combat effectively an ingrained muscular habit. It will not be long, however, before the hand begins to lose its involuntary movement and becomes responsive to the player's control. From there the mind and hand should develop together to such a degree that at every point the use of vibrato will be regulated by the expressive demands of the music.

There is tremendous potential for variation in vibrato: in intensity, in gentleness, in warmness, in quietness, or in the most passionate outburst. If we start our vibrato from nothing, we can build it into whatever the music requires. It is the endlessness of it we are after.

IV: Tempo

So how does one approach the question of tempo? The speed on the metronome? What about emotional speed, the inner sense of flow within the tempo which creates the illusion of a speed being faster or slower? Too often people allow themselves to become side-tracked from the real issues of tempo by the more obvious measurement of time on the metronome, and in doing so leave out of their consideration of tempo the most critical element: the *sense of movement*.

The metronome is only a basic way of estimating speed; the quality of flow within any metronomic speed will always be the determining factor in the sensation of tempo. When we recognize this, we are led to look beyond the external framework of a measured speed and to search out the sense of movement in the music.

Many times I have been asked at what tempo I play a particular movement or piece and I find the very question underlines a basic lack of understanding of what creates the sensation of tempo – what makes a tempo feel like *that* tempo. One person might be able to play a passage with the slowest tempo on earth with more feeling of forward movement than someone else might have at a much quicker tempo. Even the same person will vary from day to day in his sense of speed and energy and flow, and each time an ensemble comes together to play, all of these varying factors have to adjust to each other in a thousand subtle ways – you can never bathe in the same stream twice.

Sense of speed in fast passages

It is amazing the degree to which one can sabotage the sense of speed in a passage by the frantic efforts of the mind. If we do not discipline it, the mind becomes impatient and begins to fight and work at a completely different speed from the actual speed of the music and the physical time it requires, and we then end up with every fast passage sounding as if we were being chased by a bull.

It is not necessary to inject hysteria into every fast passage just because the note values are fast. Quick notes usually have more time than one thinks. Even in those passages where the music *does* need to sound breathless or impatient, the conscious sensation of speed should be something the player injects intentionally into it for musical reasons – it should never be there as a matter of course. The conscious sensation of speed is only *one* aspect of rapid movement. Misplaced anxiety or impatience only results in a feeling of chaos, and over-reaction to high speed in fast passages robs the music of the great variety of mood it should have.

At any speed the notes must have a feeling of being filled out with whatever mood or quality of expression that passage requires – some fast passages may even have a feeling of laziness in the way they are played. If we neglect the present out of anxious anticipation for the future (clipping the life of one note short, in manner or speed just because we are worried about the next), we shall be missing something all the time. Thinking one jump ahead destroys the living moment of the present. The greater the speed in a passage of music, the slower we need to think. There are some exceptions to this, but by and large it is the best way to approach a fast passage, because the quicker the notes go, the more the mind wants to rush ahead to be there to open the door for the next note or group of notes. Only by training ourselves to think more slowly within a quick tempo, will we be able to live the fullest emotional value of each note.

The right attitude of mind towards speed is especially important when there are quicker notes set between notes of longer values. Look at the principal tune in the first movement of the Elgar Concerto:

First mov't., bars 15–22

Even though the quavers have relatively less time, we must never let ourselves be misled psychologically into letting them feel less important than their longer brothers. If the musical line is to retain its beautiful unhurried flow, their sense of leisure must remain equivalent to the sense of leisure of the notes with longer values – they are only short in metronomic length, not in their emotional life. (You may live to be ninety, and a butterfly may live only a few weeks, yet the sense of leisure in its short life could be the same as in yours; it does not know that, because somebody else lives ninety years, its life span is, by comparison, relatively short.) Under conditions of tranquillity, short notes in a passage can feel just as unhurried as long ones.

Energy and the sense of speed

The feeling of speed generated by a passage of quick notes is really more a question of the amount of energy or leisure – the *sense* of energy or leisure – which one injects into the tread of the fingers and the intensity of the bow stroke. There are many different ways of playing fast notes: one fast passage may have a hard brilliance with sharply articulated finger action, while another passage at the same speed could have a gently rippling quality with a completely different tread in the fingers. You can illustrate this to yourself by playing the two passages from the Dvořák Concerto quoted below and comparing the feel of the quick notes in the first passage with the feel of the equally quick notes in the second passage:

First mov't., bars 123–6

Second mov't., bar 69

While the notes in both passages move at very nearly the same speed, those in the first example have a finger energy that should be completely absent from those in the second example: the latter are pure arabesque, almost sad in spite of their speed.

Sense of continuity in slow playing

Just as we should have the ability in fast passages to give the appearance that the notes are perhaps even slower than we are playing, so we should have the ability in slow passages to create the sensation of forward flow in spite of what is, in reality, a very slow tempo. What creates the feeling of forward flow in slow playing is a sense of *continuity*. One wants to achieve the same sense of continuity in slow playing as in fast, but this is often more difficult to attain because one feels somehow compelled to make an *effort* to control the sound and speed; in the end it begins to sound as if one is pushing *against* the music instead of gliding *upon* it.

There are many senses of movement and speed, and many degrees of resistance in the flow of any movement – so much depends on the face the slow passage or movement wears. Some adagio movements, like the slow movement of the Haydn C major Concerto, can be pregnant with an andante feeling, a gentle forward flow like a Sunday morning stroll; and in that type of 'slowness' we must not let ourselves get stuck in a sort of congealed adagio. The same is true in a simple piece like *The Swan*: it is the slowness of *feel*, not the actual speed, that counts when you play it. Even something as apparently motionless as the opening of the Adagio in the Beethoven D major Sonata must have a flow which sustains the contours of the line through the inevitability of the pulse.

In order to allow the music to flow and unfold, the mind must embrace a larger sense of relativity between the notes – a feeling of moving *through* each successive note as it becomes a part of the larger line, rather than a grasping at each note as an isolated event. This very sense of moving through the notes allows one space for the seemingly contradictory possibility of dwelling upon a particular note when there are musical reasons for stressing it rhythmically – the flow of the line enlarging to embrace the stressed note without disrupting the general sense of continuity.

The flow of the slowest river is not an effort, and yet the sense of forward movement and continuity is spellbinding.

Shape in slow playing

The slower the feel of the music is, the greater the need for big lines and complete shapes. It is important to recognize this, because slowness can entice us into letting each note exist as an entity in itself. When that happens we begin to feel stuck and lose our sense of direction and line. To counter this, we need to develop the ability to embrace many notes, however slow, within the contours of the musical shape – but first we must be able to see the contours and the shape.

To see the contours and the bigger line in a slow passage or piece, it is often necessary to step back, as it were – to do the musical equivalent of what we often do for visual objects. For instance, if you wanted to see St Paul's Cathedral, you would not start out by standing just a foot or so away; you would step back, perhaps several hundred feet, until you could see the complete outline of the structure. Having got the sense of contour from a distance, you could then go closer and marry the finer detail with what was left in your mind's eye of the big shape. In music you can use the same technique: if you feel yourself beginning to stick in a slow passage and find that your sense of musical direction starts to become heavy or wayward, try playing the passage quite a bit faster (just as an exercise) – this achieves the aural equivalent of stepping back.

When you do this, you will find that the big shapes begin to stand out, and give you a greater understanding of the contours – how they flow into, or contrast starkly against one another. From there you can return by degrees to the slow tempo the music requires, and still retain your sense of shape and flow. The slower a piece goes, the more you need to do this kind of aural 'stepping back'. When people get stuck in sarabandes and other slow movements, it is usually only because they have lost their sense of movement and direction and can no longer see the contour of the big line, sense its shape, or feel its continuity of flow. Again the sense of movement one creates in any piece or passage, fast or slow, is really more important as a musical factor than actual metronomic speed, because the feeling of the rightness or wrongness of a tempo is, in the end, a question of the emotional speed *within* that tempo.

V: Free play and order in rhythm

Everything in the world has a free play of rhythm, but that free play rests upon a foundation of order. In music this foundation grows out of a highly developed sense of rhythmic strength and accuracy. That is why persons of great taste and artistic ability can give the appearance of being free rhythmically without ever being erratic; freedom is never erratic when it grows out of the rhythmic logic of the music.

Everything operates according to its law. You can have the most varied rhythmic landscape, with every quality in it, and yet all the countless proportions will add up if they operate within the laws of its particular nature. Within any framework a phrase can have a breathtaking sense of freedom and still have discipline. That is what is meant by *real* rhythm, not just 1–2–3–4, but what unfolds from within that; the rhythm that comes out of the rhythm, the sense of burning pulse and energy, the gentle curving – whatever is needed to give the musical shape its logic. Those who play the cello in particular need to develop this deeper understanding of rhythm because of their crucial role as the generating bass in many ensembles: it is an enormous responsibility, for they hold in their hands the key to the whole rhythmic strength and life of the ensemble.

It is true, of course, that people who play evenly, but without grace, will sound mechanical. But, on the other hand, those people who play unevenly just for the sake of sounding free, and with no real understanding of the inner logic of the rhythm, will end up with a rhythmic 'freedom' which is warped and distorted. Playing mechanically is bad, but playing on personal whim alone opens up the worst possible avenue of development, and those who defend it on the grounds of 'musicality' are relying on either an uninformed musicality or no musicality at all.

The 'spine' of rhythm

We string players in particular tend to be weak when it comes to rhythm; we pull things about and twist them this way and that often without any real understanding of the relation between the inner core, or 'spine', of the rhythm and what we are doing. We forget that strength of rhythm must be our *starting* point – if we lose even one per cent of the discipline in a rhythmically tight passage, we have lost it all. Even in music which is rhythmically less tightly disciplined, there can be a gentle persistence of the rhythm that is so terribly in time that it is tantalizing. It is important to understand that there are rhythms which derive their energy and their very being from the conscious presence of the impulse of the beat, and there are rhythms which have an absolute logic without even implying the beats from which they arise.

Even silence is incorporated in the whole scheme of rhythm – it is the rhythm of space and timing. There is the pause which is generated out of the rhythm and becomes a form of tension, there is the pause which allows the rhythm to settle and recompose itself, and there is the pause which contains within itself the inevitable psychological moment of birth, of what happens out of it. At all times sound and silence involve a sense of drama, and an understanding of the extremes of lyrical and dynamic form.

Ultimately it comes down once again to the logic of emotional shapes: it comes down, too, to the way those shapes play against each other, or unfold out of one another, to create the larger landscape of the work of art. It is never simply a matter of playing with blind rhythmic accuracy; nothing can ever be really accurate if it is out of step with the inner logic of the music, the inner logic of the emotional structure of the line. It is freedom within the boundaries set by the rhythmic spine that we should want, the minute bending of the line to either side of the spine to allow the musical sentence to develop.

Rhythmic spine and rubato

The idea of bending is beautiful when it is used at the right time and to the proper degree. Thoughts and moods in music have tremendous variation in their rhythmic realization, and the bending of the line can become a loosening factor which gives the rhythm of the whole musical structure its life and logic. It is not necessary to move very far from the spine to have that variation and to let those moods happen – it is never a matter of being metronomically miles out.

But we must never forget that *before* we bend something we must first start with a rhythmic line which is pure and untampered with by the whims of the individual. This is a universal law of all the arts. You cannot have a beautiful rubato unless you first have an understanding and command of the rhythmic foundation which provides the point of departure for that rubato. Only then will whatever rubato you do (assuming you are musical) contain within itself an inner logic which will unfold to reveal the beauty of the line.

Eleven
The Unbroken Circle of Imagination and Receiving

Imagination which finds its source in the music is the beginning of all creativity on the cello.

Use your fantasy all the time – do not be afraid to go wrong with it. Even if it should go wrong, it is still healthier than something that is without fantasy. But always remember, too, that true artistic imagination does not consist in inventing the musical sense of a passage according to a personal whim, but rather in discovering and demonstrating the sense already inherent in the music itself.

When one talks about fantasy and imagination, one is not talking about free flights of fancy outside the score. There are many ways of fulfilling emotionally what one sees on paper without recomposing what the composer has written. Our role rather is to discover the composer's intention through obeying what he has given us and attaching our fantasies to that. It does not begin with us – the fantasies and emotions within the score are endless, and *they* must be our starting point.

The truth is, we often do not realize the magnitude of what we are standing before, and the importance of bringing ourselves into alignment with it. We are too often prone to overlay our own personalities on the music, injecting into it whatever qualities are in our hearts and letting our own fantasy run riot (it is like having an opinion before understanding what the opinion is about). This often stands in the way of our discovering the even greater musical fantasy we could develop if we would let the music mould us. We need instead to develop the ability to recognize the music in the purity of its own world and have the courage, without interfering with what is in the score, to relate our fantasy to *it*. It takes real courage and will-power at times to stand apart from ourselves in this way, but it is never enough to imagine that we are making contact with the music emotionally if we have not first reached out to discover the nature of *its* emotion.

There are many ways of doing this: one way is to play a phrase many times, each time with a different face, a different sentiment. But when you do this as an exercise, always keep within the context of the mood and the basic language of that composer and that work; there is no point in saying, 'Well, the composer wrote *piano*, so I'll try it *forte*.' There are a million sentiments within any language, but you must not get your languages mixed up. One can be inspired to play a passage or a work many different ways without stepping out of the basic language of the music: this always remains the same, but one's musical insight and inspiration, one's musical imagination and spontaneity, will be slightly different from one performance to another.

Aligning oneself with the language of the composer and the spirit of the music is never the limiting thing some people imagine it to be. The more languages we can speak, the less limited we are; the more great authors we have read, the broader the background for our own thinking. Surely then we shall be richer if we allow the great composers of our art to draw us into *their* realms of musical inspiration. Any work of great stature can only widen the scope of our imagination and our whole musical being if we are prepared to stand before it and let its heart open up a vision in our hearts, a vision we can then begin to recreate in our own playing.

'Receiving'

As you reach out with your fantasy, you must learn to

'receive' as well. The ability to receive what you do, to discriminate and determine to what degree the sounds you are creating coincide with the imagination which gave them birth, is the other side of the creative coin. It is only when you receive that you can feed back into the creative mechanism and complete the circle.

Too often receiving is blocked and tremendous imperfections are passed over by the ear because players have become so wrapped up in the physical sensation of playing the cello that they have not really heard what they have created. You cannot have a physical experience on the cello that is nothing more than just that: the physical experience and the musical vision must hold hands.

In order to go beyond the purely physical sensation of playing the cello, or the intellectualizing of it, we must receive everything about our playing – the quality and texture of the sound, the shape of the line as we create it, the intonation, the bowing articulations; the complete picture. If we do not, we shall only feed back to our creative mechanism an incomplete, and therefore blurred and inaccurate image. Always remember that the gap between what we do and what we would not accept in someone else's playing is the measure of our deafness to our own playing, of our inability to *receive* in the fullest sense. ('Listening' and 'receiving' are, to me, two different things. Receiving is taking in the whole picture and is something which should never stop. Listening, on the other hand, is the equivalent of looking: it is when you decide to focus sharply on a particular item to the exclusion of all else around it in order to understand something about it more completely. In music, it is pinpointing the attention on some particular aspect of your or your partner's playing within the larger context of receiving. Therefore listening has various degrees of intensity whilst travelling within the broader stream of receiving – it is a vital part of one's practice and rehearsals – but the greater the ear's ability to receive in a complete and unbroken continuity, the greater will be its power of pinpointing.)

Conceptualizing and discrimination

Imagination and receiving go hand in hand; they are the outward and inward thrusts in a great unending circle. Imagination leads us to conceptualize, to form some idea in our minds of what we want to create: receiving what we have created causes us to discriminate about what we have heard in terms of our concept and to feed this back into the imagination. Thus conceptualizing is the child of the imagination, and discriminating is the child of receiving.

Obviously, the concept must be there before we can discriminate about what we are receiving: receiving has to relate to something. If it does not, the ears will tend to turn off and cease to receive properly because they have not been given a concept beforehand to relate their receiving to. It all depends upon our ability to receive in a *connected* sense; of our having a concept (which has grown out of the imagination *vis-à-vis* the music) and of our relating all that we hear to that concept. It does not matter that your opinion may change with the passage of time and with increased musical maturity – one would certainly hope to evolve in one's thinking – but the important thing is to have an opinion which, if nothing else, can become a starting point for further growth and deeper understanding. When we receive in this connected way, *then* we will be in a position to make demands upon our technique so that what we have visualized musically can become a physical (aural) reality. (Too often, I fear, there are not enough demands made: the notes of the various lines are carried like a load of baggage, chucked into the boot and off you go!)

When we learn to work in this more complete way, our emotional commitment on the cello will be on a healthier footing. We *should* have commitment and passion in what we are playing, but the discipline of the mind and ear must harness the passion so that it does not run wild and make a mockery of the music. It is never sufficient to play on whatever emotion happens to come to hand and be happy with the feel of it; the mind and the ear – the imagination and the ability to receive – cannot be kept outside. Receiving enables the imagination and the physical to hold hands, and not grope blindly for each other in the dark.

Receiving in the wider context

'Oneness' in our own playing grows out of receiving the sounds we are making. But there is a wider receiving still, a receiving that embraces every other part that is playing alongside us in the music, where the 'one' within our own playing is so complete that it can be part of the larger 'one' which is the concerted work.

Completeness in our own part can only be arrived at through an understanding of the whole – of how our instrument fits with others, of how our lines must be conceived in relation to the other parts around us. There are, for instance, many passages in our chamber and sonata repertoire where the cello part engages in a wonderful dialogue with the other part or parts; but the whole sense of dialogue will not come about if we get so determined about our own part, receiving only our own playing and indulging in that little world, that we become oblivious to the fact that our choice of colours and textures, our vibrato, the way we bend the line rhythmically – all of which may have sounded fine on their own – is misfiring in terms of the complete musical picture.

Even while our mind is on the cello part, we cannot divorce it from the other lines it is related to. Our involvement in our own part must include at the same time a much wider involvement with our partners and with the complete musical picture. We must be able to receive their parts along with our own and then have the discipline to develop what we are doing in terms of those parts.

Receiving on a wider level does not mean that we must become detached and emotionally uninvolved in our playing, but it does mean that we are going to have to shed that which tends to be foremost in most people's minds, namely 'playing the cello'. Even if we are playing the most passionate or most difficult passage on earth, we are still a part of the brickwork. If we do not understand this, and relate what we are doing to the total concept, then we will follow our own part into very false realms.

Twelve
Ensemble Playing

Playing chamber music is like embarking upon an expedition.

Unlike the 'guided tour' of orchestra playing, each member in an ensemble is required to have a full understanding of the general plan of the musical journey. This understanding must be so complete in the mind of each player that he is at all times clearly aware of how his, and all the other individual lines, fit into the total scheme. Chamber musicians have to learn to discriminate and make the appropriate demands on every part: where there is lack of recognition of all the strands that go together to weave a piece of music, there will be lack of discrimination as to the role of the various parts (and then the strands, because they are not doing anything in particular, will tend to get in one another's way).

Understanding the whole

If you were an actor in a play, you would want first to read through the whole play and have a good idea of what the other parts were doing, and what your relation to them was, before you began to work on your own part and develop it. And when you began to learn your lines, you would want to be familiar enough with the other parts that they could sit there in your mind as a backcloth against which to practise your part.

In chamber music the score is our script, and a thorough understanding of it is no less important to what we are doing if our individual parts are going to make sense. If we try to learn our parts in isolation from any knowledge of the other parts, or if, when we come to rehearse with our partners, we play with our nose so much in our own part that we cannot get the full impact of the other lines, then we cannot have much to identify with and relate to in our own part.

It is only by understanding the *entirety* of a work that we can keep the logic of our own line whilst contributing to the logic of the whole. We need not fear that we will lose our individuality by relating to others in the ensemble: good ensemble playing does not rule out individuality any more than good acting rules out individuality. It is simply setting a bigger universe for the individuality to move about in. And when it operates within the laws of that larger universe, true individuality is never chaotic, never erratic: that is its great beauty.

Characterization in ensemble playing

When the roles of the various parts are not clear in the players' minds, it is terribly easy for one player to let himself be carried into the emotional stream of another player's part. Avoiding this demands not only the ability to discriminate, to know when a particular line is going to have to stand out and what the other parts are going to have to do to let it stand out; it demands as well a sense of characterization – an awareness of the diversity of the nature of each part and the role it is playing. Only by establishing their own sense of identity can the parts keep clear of the emotional stream of the others, even while they are at the same time working together to produce a unified whole.

This delineation of roles and characterization is something we take for granted in opera. On the opera stage it is not uncommon to have a scene where a couple is singing a love duet while another character is singing spiteful comments about the two in the love duet. Though musically it all has to fit together in perfect ensemble, the lovers must pretend not to notice what the other is singing – or even that he is singing it. If the singers were to lose sight of the function of their individual roles and let themselves get carried away into the other character's emotional stream, they would not only muddy the waters for each other but would also undermine the strength of their own individual parts.

On an instrumental level we have an equivalent of this kind of portrayal in much chamber music. One player may have a loving tune while another player has some articulated notes set against it; and while playing together as a unified whole, they must still keep the individual characteristics of each part separate and intact. In the Beethoven String Quartet, Op. 59, No. 2, for example, a sublimely reverent line in the upper strings, with a superb expressive dialogue between the two violins, is set off by a tight, hauntingly fateful staccato figure in the cello:

Molto Adagio: bars 92–5

In this case the character of the cello part is particularly difficult to maintain because it sits under such persuasive violin parts. Yet it would be fatal to the musical outcome if the cellist were to let himself get sucked into the emotional stream of the others.

There are countless examples in the chamber music repertoire where the various instruments must depict extreme opposites of colour, mood and characterization. Each time the players must be so aware of how their own

113

particular part fits against the other part or parts that they can maintain the integrity of its character and thereby fulfil the whole.

The importance of the bass line and middle voices in ensemble playing

In all ensemble playing one should build from the bass line, for it is the lifeline of a piece of music. Yet musicians often become so mesmerized by the top line that they leave the bass to follow along like a shadow. Perhaps they fear that if they give it too much attention, it will get in the way and detract from the top line – or perhaps they never give it any real thought at all. Whatever the reason, it often ends up being used merely as a little bolster-upper for the treble and is denied its existence as a line in its own right. (This attitude frequently goes so far that when the bass does take over the tune from the top, players forget to let it do an equal job of portraying.)

To counteract this tendency to underplay the bass, it is often a good idea in any ensemble (and I include in this cello/piano duos, where the pianist often finds himself responsible for several voice lines at the same time) to play the bass line on its own and make sense of it as a complete part. By doing this one will begin to understand its logic and growth, to invest it with its own sense of purpose as an independent line in its own right and not treat it as just a 'filling in'.

The upper lines need the bass in order to be shown to advantage. In fact, until the bass has been given its rightful emphasis, one has never really heard the tune in its proper setting, for the quality of the bass line in any ensemble will underpin the upper lines and help to put them in relief. In any piece of chamber music we must ask ourselves what sort of life the bass line needs in order to provide the upper line with the right foundation or foil; depending on the way the bass sets it off, the life of the upper line can be shown up in totally different lights or dimensions.

Nowhere is the bass line more important than in Baroque music. It is for this reason that ensembles should seek out the very finest musicians for the continuo cello part. If the continuo cellist is a dull, unimaginative player, he is going to suck the life out of the ensemble and the music. A sensitive, imaginative cellist, however, will not only give life to all that goes on in the upper lines, but will successfully shape the architecture of the whole. (In this respect, the continuo cellist fulfils a role similar to that of a good conductor.)

While it is important to win people away from the obvious tune and get them to build from the bass, it is equally important to give proper attention to the middle voices in an ensemble. I never understand the lack of investigation into the meaning of these parts – their character, their function as related to the whole – for these are what give shape and texture to the whole.

This holds true as well for cello/piano duos, where the inner voices in the piano part are often neglected or completely ignored. To sharpen their attentiveness to these lines, cellists should ask the pianist to play each line separately (adding the cello part first to one line and then to another). By focusing attention on these less obvious voices for a while, they will begin to hear with greater completeness *all* the strands that are woven together to make the fabric of the music. When they get back to the tune again, they will hear it with new ears. By recognizing the personality and the role of the inner parts they will perceive this tune in a different light and it will show to greater advantage.

Chamber musicians should always approach the various lines in their music in the same way a great conductor approaches an orchestral piece. Having already formulated his concept from the score and imagined it in his mind's ear – every line, every colour, the blocks of sound, the counterpoints – he will then discriminate in rehearsal and pinpoint what is wrong and know what has to be done to put it right.

The Cello

Intonation within the ensemble

Intonation is not the absolute that many people often imagine it to be. For the string player there are not twelve notes within the octave, but an infinite number. Depending on the harmonic setting and the textures which are put against a note, one may have to move the finger quite a distance (within any one pitch) in order to 'fine tune' the note and enable it to fit in with its tonal environment.

You can prove this to yourself by playing an e on the D string against your open A string and getting the interval perfectly in tune (make sure you have tuned your strings well before trying this). Then, holding the same e, play the open G and C strings against it. You will find this second chord wildly out of tune. You can reverse the process if you want by retuning your e to the G and C strings and then (without moving your finger) playing that same e against your open A. You will have the same out-of-tune results against the A this time. The fact is that when you change the harmonic environment of a note, the note itself will have to be adjusted to fit the new tonality (and you may be surprised to see just how great the actual space of adjustment is). It is this kind of tuning I am referring to when I talk about 'fine tuning'.

Sequential, or melodic, pitch, incidentally, can be just as relative. Try playing a G major scale up to fourth position on the A string and make it as perfectly in tune as you can. Then test your f sharp against your open D string to see what you think about its 'in-tuneness'. Assuming you have a good ear, it probably *was* in tune during the scale in terms of the melodic sequence it was in; but against the harmonic implications of the open D, and the implications of the different texture as well, a fairly sizeable adjustment is demanded in order to have it in tune in this different context.

'Basic intonation', i.e. carefully spaced fingers, even in a relatively perfected state, is only the first part of the journey. It is when the notes you play are put in the

116

harmonic and textural context of the complete piece of music that the additional fine adjustments begin to make themselves apparent. (In something like the Bach Suites, where you are completely on your own, you can 'fine tune' only in so far as it relates to itself, but 'fine tuning' in solo playing is a limited thing. The term really only takes on its fullest meaning when one is playing with others. This is why fine tuning becomes so crucial to good ensemble playing.)

It is only when you are with your partners that the variations of colour, texture, harmony, vibrato, etc., can suggest to you, and demand from you, the fine tuning that fulfils all the other musical aspects. The very texture of any note you play should already suggest to your hand a fine, almost imperceptible retuning to allow it to fit with its musical surroundings. Different dynamics, different textures, different balances, different vibratos should all cause your hand to react accordingly.

With other string players we can have the most perfect intonation of all because all players will be able to control their pitch to the finest degree. But this also demands that players control their vibrato with the same degree of exactitude, because two notes can be exactly in tune and yet not sound in tune if the players have different vibratos which are out of step with each other. Our approach to intonation and fine tuning will need to become more flexible when we play with other instruments. When we play with piano, for instance, it is *we* who will have to do all the adjusting. Many notes can sound perfectly in tune on the cello alone and yet sound out of tune when a particular chord is put against them by the piano – even with a well-tuned piano. In these situations it is always up to the cellist to adjust his pitch in order to make the whole sound in tune. In a similar way, we have to be equally quick to make minute adjustments in pitch when we play with wind instruments. Although their pitch can be modified somewhat, wind players have less flexibility in pitch than do string players. Our whole approach to intonation requires the kind of sensitivity of ear and flexibility of hand we have already talked about. When the ear 'lives in the hand', and when we receive all that we and our partners are creating, then the kind of fine tuning and pitch modification we have been talking about will happen instinctively.

Colour and texture vis-à-vis other instruments

There is in all of us a tendency to stop short and fail to visualize what another sound from another instrument is going to do to our own sound. We get caught up in a kind of unrealistic mental set that says that whatever sounds good on our own must, by definition, sound good at all times and in all situations. But this is a deadening attitude because it causes the ears to close down both in the practice room and in the rehearsal.

Awareness of the importance of colour and texture in ensemble playing creates in the musician a tremendous mental and emotional agility (and, it follows, a concomitant agility in the handling of sound on one's instrument). The development of this agility is essential for the creation of a wide spectrum of sound qualities *vis-à-vis* other instruments and an understanding of how these sound qualities can be used to set off the various lines in the best way. If we think of sound colour and texture in terms of the whole, then the way we develop our colours and textures in an ensemble will be within the context of the qualities inherent in the instruments of the ensemble, and in terms of the unique sound qualities which can result from the conjoining of those instruments.

Experiment some time with the sound of your cello against that of another instrument. Try playing your cello against a violin in a duo, and then have a clarinettist or a flautist play the violin part on his instrument; you will immediately notice that the sound of the cello becomes very different with each instrument as the colours and textures which are set against it, or with which it blends, change. Or try sustaining a note on the cello and then add a clarinet, then take it away and add it again; by doing that you will discover how the sound of the cello appears to alter as the clarinet is added or taken away. Just as colours appear to change as they are placed next to different colours, so sounds also appear differently to our ears depending on what is put next to them.

By playing with other instruments we can learn a great deal about our own instrument and develop greater command of colour and texture, of vibrato and intonation. Knowing that a clarinettist, for example, will not be able to modify his sound with vibrato to the extent that a cellist can, a cellist is going to have to choose straighter colours when he plays with a clarinettist. This is especially true in unison passages like the opening of the Beethoven Trio, Op. 11, where the sound of the one instrument has to sit in the lap of the other: the cellist can ruin the whole sound if he plays with a big, warm, wide vibrato. He has to choose instead a vibrato which is much more contained in order to match the sound of the clarinet. At other times, of course, and in other musical situations, a cellist may want to choose contrasting colours and use his vibrato in a way that will set his lines off from the clarinet.

These are all reasons why the aural imagination cannot stop with one's own part. Other factors have to be a part of your thinking when you are practising and rehearsing and making your decisions about the colours and textures you are going to use to develop your line. You cannot be content with just making your part sound good on its own because, in the final analysis, it is not on its own; your one part is not the end product, it is part of something larger.

Practising with the whole canvas in view

Even on our own in the practice room we have to have this larger vision, a vision broad enough to enable us to imagine even what a note should *not* be on its naked own. This requires both a knowledge of the score and an imaginative understanding of sound. Take, for example, the first Allegro in the Beethoven C major Sonata:

The nature of this music is determined by the really brittle keyboard octaves, so in this case the cello must find a way to match the piano. This can best be achieved by taking advantage of the harder-edged sound of the open A string, yet I rarely meet a cellist who does not shift up on the D string in this passage. When I suggest the use of the A string to students, they almost shudder at the thought.

Now I understand this in a way, because the strident sound of the A string when hit in this way on its own is not particularly pleasant. (This is not to imply that the A string is always strident. It is necessarily *made* strident here by the nature of the bowing attacks and the dynamic the music requires.) But what these students do not understand is that the sound they make on the cello will not be perceived as that sound when it comes together with the piano's sound. What the cellist wants to do with his sound in this passage is to highlight the percussiveness and power of the piano, to unite with him in creating the sensation of a marvellous unison *tutti*. Together the two instruments will add up to a new sound which serves the character of this music, however pleasing or 'right' a different choice of string colour might be on its own on the cello.

Another example of the transformation of the sound of one instrument when it is joined with the sound of another instrument (and a good illustration of how misleading it can be for one single-mindedly to develop one's sound on one's own) comes in the opening of the slow movement of the Brahms Double Concerto.

When each player is practising on his own he instinctively tries to make the whole richness of the sound (which Brahms intended as the finished product) come out of his one instrument. Forgetting that he is going to have a partner in the creation of this passage, he tries to do it all by himself. The result, when the two 'complete' sounds come together, is that they do battle with each other. The clash of vibratos, of resonances, of the two sounds getting in each other's way, that one hears in most performances is all for the want of the individual discipline we have been talking about – the ability to see one's own line as part of a larger article.

We have to bear in mind that the composer chose to write this passage in unison not so much to have the sound of two instruments, but in order to create a new colour out of the *fusion* of the two instruments. The emphasis is upon a colour which neither the cello nor the violin possesses on its own, and the two partners should be striving together for a portrayal of that sound.

In any ensemble one has to accept that if a composer chose to write for a particular combination of instruments, it must have had a purpose. It is up to us to use our instruments in a way that helps to uncover that purpose. Musical partnerships can be marvellously fulfilling precisely because the different instruments inspire each other and take each other into realms of colours and textures which are denied one on one's own. But this requires of us a heightened awareness of the way colours and textures interact when we play with others. It is something which should never desert us, or our creative endeavours on our instrument. The vision of these wider concepts must follow us around like our own shadow – into the practice room, the rehearsal, and wherever we play. It must be so much a part of us that nothing we do is divorced from the whole.

Thirteen
Playing with Piano

When we play with piano we have to be very much aware of the qualities and characteristics which belong to the nature of that instrument and understand how to use the cello's qualities and characteristics in relation to them. Even two such disparate instruments must, in the end, result in sounds, colours, textures and articulations which are either perfectly blended with or (depending on the music) perfectly contrasted to one another.

I mention later, in my chapter on repertoire, that from Beethoven onward there has hardly been a great composer who has not written for the cello and piano as a duo, and I refer to the inspiration composers must have drawn from the great variety of colours, textures and contrapuntal scope afforded them by this kind of a musical partnership, from the fusion of two such diverse instruments into a single larger unit. But how does one work with these vastly different instruments in a way which allows the expressive colour and texture potentials to be realized?

Recognition has to come first before anything else can follow, for only when each partner is able to recognize what both he and the other are doing can he relate his sound to that of the other. From there the two of them can discuss the relative merits of what each has done and work out what they feel is correct in terms of the music – but without recognition in the first place, each partner is flying blind in his own world of sound.

Neither partner can indulge in his own part to the exclusion of the other, even when he is on his own. There is little point, for instance, in the cellist going into realms of sound where the pianist cannot hope to follow – realms which have nothing to do with the music and which are little more than 'celloisms' – if the pianist is going to come in later with the same theme or figuration. In the opening of the Beethoven A major Sonata, for example, the cellist must know ahead of time that the nature of the piano is not going to let it have a juicy slide up to the second note when it comes in with the theme and, since the two statements of the theme must match, thus forego that possibility.

In the same way, in the opening of the final movement of the same sonata, the cellist will need to anticipate in advance the slight articulations within the legato which the pianist is going to have when he comes in later on by underlining each note slightly within the legato. Whenever one is on one's own, one has to make a bigger circle around the imagination, which includes the logic of what will happen to the partner who has yet to enter.

This kind of awareness and recognition of what the other instrument is doing, and *can* do, has to permeate all your playing together; everything the one plays has to relate to the other in a way that will lead to balance in the partnership. Granted, one is not going to have all the answers on the first play-through, but by the time it gets to the performance stage one should not be hearing mismatches of sound and intent which should have been recognized and solved in the earliest rehearsals.

Learning from the piano

We cellists cannot afford to blot out of our minds the strokes and textures which the nature of the piano can suggest to us: in fact, we are so often going to have to take our cue from the piano that we must heighten our awareness of what the piano is doing. Fine pianists have a broad command of strokes and articulations ranging from a wonderful illusion of legato to the hardest, most brittle attacks; the string player must be able to go to those extremes – and also have every shade in between. It is not enough to be satisfied with just 'playing the cello' and remain ignorant of the wider possibilities open to one.

The first two Beethoven Sonatas, Op. 5, are prime examples of where the cellist cannot afford to be ignorant of the natural articulations of the piano. In the opening of the F major Sonata, for instance, the cellist will have to play with a sound almost devoid of vibrato in order to match the purity of the piano's sound:

And later in the same sonata, when he begins the Allegro, his stroke on the accompanying figure must match perfectly with the left hand of the piano:

Another example of how important it is for the cellist to match his strokes to the pianist's articulations occurs at the end of the first movement of the Beethoven A major Sonata when the cellist joins with the pianist's octaves in the final statement of the theme. The nature of the pianist's articulations, imposed upon him by the octaves in both hands, must dictate the nature of the cellist's stroke. It is

125

pointless for the cellist to slur his notes in a manner which will undermine the strength of the pianist's octave statement and make a mockery of the forceful intent of the passage. He must instead find a way to play separate strokes which are not disjointed and which will match up with and become a part of the pianist's articulations within an overall concept of legato.

In the last movement of the Brahms E minor Sonata, the cellist must match his stroke to the piano so perfectly that, in effect, he becomes another finger of the pianist. This fugue has to grow out of a basic germ, and unless this germ is expressed by a unified idea of stroke between the partners, then the whole sense of unity in the fugue and the whole stature of the movement will be ruined.

The Mendelssohn B-flat Sonata provides another good example of where the cellist has to become *part* of the pianist's stroke. And again, we have to widen our concepts of our own techniques to achieve this:

It is not enough for the cellist just to give a little extra dig with the bow and feel satisfied with the sensation of the physical effort. To make his sound fit with the articulated block chords in the piano, the cellist is going to have to lift slightly at either end of the bow in order to let in a little 'daylight' and match the articulations of the piano. Now most cellists will automatically lift at the frog, but rarely does one hear a cellist lift with the same sense of spacing and strength at the point. The end result is that only every second note in the cello line fits with the piano, and the ones in between blur through the piano's articulations. Admittedly, this is a much easier articulation to achieve on the piano: the pianist in this instance is making *equal* movements and does not have the physical differences of up-bows and down-bows to contend with, whilst the cellist must make very *unequal* movements at the frog and point to create the same sound. But because it is difficult on the cello, this illustration serves to underline the point that the very nature of our instrument can at times lead us into being blinded to other possibilities of sound and articulation which we can achieve with a little effort and imagination. By trying to meet the demands of the piano, we have an opportunity to widen our command of our instrument. In the end we should be able instinctively to match any articulation of the piano on the cello.

Even when not played at their best, many piano articulations such as these provide a germ for one's thinking, because it is harder in these cases for the pianist to go wrong. And even if the pianist is wrong, the cellist cannot come in with the same figure articulated completely differently – what the two partners do has to be unified. You do not have to accept what the pianist does – you can discuss it with him in rehearsal and work out alternative possibilities – but in actual performance, if one player articulates a passage in a certain way on his instrument and the second player does it slightly differently when the parts swap over, *both* will be reduced to being wrong.

On the performance platform your awareness has to be so automatic that whatever your partner does, right or wrong, you will reflexively react to it and will play your part in a way that puts a complete face on the music. It needs great wisdom and experience not to spoil something when your partner has handed it to you wrongly, but it is precisely at that point that you have to counter the primitive instinct to 'put it right'. There is always a moment when you can get the music back on the track if you nurse it properly. You can argue with your partner about the passage later, if you want, but the real test of awareness and spontaneous reflex comes in these unexpected situations under fire. The whole point to be made is that the way in which you choose to use your cello against the piano is based on recognition of what the two parts are doing.

If I seem to stress the responsibilities (and weaknesses) of the cellist overmuch, it is for two reasons (apart from the fact that this book is, after all, about the cello): first, because cellists frequently think of themselves as 'soloists' and tend to ignore the piano part as a 'mere accompaniment' (therefore closing their minds to any need for recognition of what the pianist has played); and secondly, because many of the articulations and textures in the duo repertoire, as I have been stressing throughout, are dictated by the nature of the piano and are therefore an important factor in determining what we do on the cello.

But all duo playing is a two-way street, and there is much that the pianist can learn from the cellist, and many ways in which he is going to have to adapt his sound to the cello's sound or part. To take just one of many possible illustrations: in the first movement of the Brahms E minor Sonata, at bars 145–8, the attack on the bass notes in the piano must be suggestive of a *pizzicato* answer to the cellist's *pizzicati*:

Although this same octave figure evolves later into a more legato, timpani-like stroke in the piano, for those first few preceding bars the pianist must take his cue from the pizzicato sound on the cello. The list of similar examples would be endless, but I leave this for the pianists (and cellists) to discover on their own.

One word of caution, however: the need for greater awareness of the other's part, and the need at times for one instrument to match the sound of the other, should in no way be taken to imply that all distinctions between the two instruments should be obliterated (we could not do that even if we wanted to). There are always going to be subtle differences (that, after all, was what the composer was after when he chose this particular combination), but it concerns me that one too often hears differences which go far beyond the basic natures of the two instruments and become actually wrong in terms of the musical concept.

The different uses of the cello and piano duo

So far I have referred most frequently to the sonatas of Beethoven. The reason for this is that in these sonatas the cellist is more closely bound to the piano than in any others; and Beethoven's closely-knit, more tightly structured approach to the use of the two instruments makes unwarranted cellistics look all the more out of place. His sonatas therefore provide the ultimate example of the points that have to be made regarding the duo relationship of these two instruments. However, one should not lose sight of other composers who use the instruments on other planes which are equally legitimate and fulfilling.

Chopin, for instance, while still using the instruments in the tightly structured and interrelated way Beethoven does, often likes to play off the intrinsic qualities of one instrument against the other, using the differences in the instrumental personalities to *complement* one another. For instance, when the cellist enters with the second subject in bars 61–8 of the first movement of the Chopin Sonata, he may want gently to bind the wider intervals and thus expand upon the pianist's original statement with a more vocalized approach. This kind of indulgence in one's instrumental possibilities, which might have been grossly out of place in Beethoven, can add a breath of beauty to Chopin, provided it is done with discretion and good taste.

The Cello

Later, in the *Scherzo*, the pianist finds himself with a lovely rippling effect, which serves as a background to the flowing waltz melody in the cello. Here, at bars 134–7, the basic characteristics of both instruments are used to great advantage, and neither player has to concern himself with matching or imitating:

In situations like this, even if the cellist at times indulges wrongly in his own part or instrument, it is not going to show itself up to the degree it would in Beethoven. But this bit of leeway should not lead us to overlook the fact that Chopin's music also requires tremendous discretion even while the instruments indulge more completely in their own characteristics.

Rachmaninov, in the first movement of his Cello Sonata, bars 17–21, takes the individual characteristics of the cello and piano and uses the opposite sides of their natures to make a whole:

Many other composers – Mendelssohn, Saint-Saëns, Barber and a host of others, particularly from the Romantic period onward – create their richness of score from the very diversity of the two instruments, as well as from their ability to imitate each other. The great beauty of the cello/piano repertoire lies in the many ways in which the instruments can be used against each other, and cellists should relish the opportunity of discovering this with every new composition they play.

Balance with the piano

One talks about balance in ensemble playing, and most people think one is talking about relative loudness between the partners. But balance is a far more subtle thing than a mere arranging of decibel levels between various instruments. What you put around a note determines not only the illusion of colour and texture, but also the sensation of relative loudness. A single candle in the darkness can seem very bright; but switch on an electric light next to it and it will lose all sensation of brightness.

Balance problems become especially critical between such diverse instruments as the cello and the piano. Ironically, the very diversity which so attracted composers in the first place has all too frequently dismayed performers and caused them to shrug their shoulders and abdicate responsibility for solving the problems which grow out of this diversity. They opt for the single easy solution of putting the lid down on the piano and asking the pianist to play this *duo* repertoire, with all its emotional diversity, as 'softly as possible'. But shushing the pianist is no solution at all, it is merely turning one's back on the problem. The imagination, which should thrive on the potentialities of the diverse nature of the two instruments, is then left outside of it altogether. We should instead welcome the world of possibilities that the problems of balance between the two instruments bring with them: every problem is a potential musical fulfilment begging for a good solution.

The Cello

Balance between the cello and piano, even in problematical movements like the last movement of the Brahms E minor Sonata, the last movement of the Chopin Sonata, or the Fugue at the end of the D major Sonata by Beethoven, can be achieved if the pianist and cellist know how to handle their lines. As I said earlier, it is a question of texture, of articulations, of what is put next to, or behind, or underneath the partner's note, that creates balance. It is easy enough for the 'brighter light' of the piano to eclipse the sound of the cello, but people often forget that balance is a two-way street and that there are also times when the cello, through wrong choices of textures and articulations, can muddy the waters for the piano as well.

What misleads us so often is the fact that the cello and piano often have to approach balance from opposite directions. For the cellist it is frequently a matter of clarity of stroke and texture in order that his sound can tell against that of the piano; for the pianist the problem is more likely to be related to the sheer quantity of notes he has to play (especially in Classical works on the modern piano). Often this makes it difficult for him to play softly enough or transparently enough to let the cello sound through. If one were to play composers like Beethoven on the piano of their time, it would all be beautifully clear and the problems of balance would be quite different – he actually put all those notes there in order to achieve the effect he wanted on the piano he knew. Modern pianists must be aware of this and not let themselves blindly accept the standard sound of the modern piano: it is capable of much more than most pianists imagine, and when they play music of earlier periods on a modern piano, they are going to have to stretch their imaginations and their techniques to come closer to the clarity of that original sound.

One of the greatest obstacles to good balance remains the fact that cellists often use their sound in such a limited way that it is difficult for them to relate it to the pianist's sound, or for them to have any idea of how the pianist should relate to them. This frequently comes about because cellists do not bring the piano in early enough in the learning process. Whether this is due to the 'concerto mentality' on the part of the cellist or to a reluctance on the part of the pianist to rehearse, it should nevertheless be overcome, because it is vital for the sound of *both* that even in the note-learning stages each develops his sound *with the total concept in mind*. (Pianists are just as guilty as cellists in fostering wrong attitudes towards the need for rehearsal. Many feel that if they can play their notes and stay together with the cellist, then they are doing all that can be expected of them. Whereas, in truth, in mastering that much they have only arrived at the point where serious rehearsal can begin.)

For the cellist, achieving balance means a willingness to make the kinds of demand on his technique we have already talked about. This in turn requires him to give much more attention to certain elements – choice of strings, the string textures and brightnesses, articulations – than he might otherwise find necessary on his own or with other stringed instruments. Pianists, for their part, must develop an acute awareness of how to bring out the middle voices; they must know when the bass should be underlined to give foundation, direction and clarity to the rest of the voices; and of the effect pedallings have on the mix of sound with the cello. Choice of colours, textures and attacks must always be determined by a keen understanding of the interaction of the sounds of the two instruments.

It is only when the cellist and pianist work closely together in this way that they can begin to learn and develop the whole craft of balance; only out of a real understanding of the relation between the instruments can they have all of the other qualities we have been talking about. Again, it does not necessarily have to be correct to start out with, it only has to be *integrated*. Complete integration of sounds and intent is the only basis upon which a discussion of balance, or of any other question, for that matter, can begin.

The fallacy of the 'accompanist'

Before we leave this chapter on the musical partnership of cello and piano, I would like to comment once again on the terrible fallacy of the keyboard player as 'accompanist' following the so-called 'cello soloist'. String players must get over the idea that when they play with piano they are the 'soloists'. What can be more absurd than to see a string player come out on the platform to play a sonata by Beethoven, Debussy, Rachmaninov or Brahms, and play from memory while the pianist plays from music? Or to see the cellist's name in large print on the programme and the pianist's in small? What would we think if a string quartet came out and one of the players played from memory and behaved as the 'soloist'? This attitude in cello/piano duo playing destroys the whole idea of togetherness of purpose: it shows disrespect for one's partner and ignorance of the nature of the music. Psychologically it is wrong for the public as well, for it leads them to wrongly regard one player as the 'soloist' and the other as the 'accompanist', and gives rise to the concept of the pianist as a sort of secondary figure.

Still more important, from a musical point of view, pianists should never be forced into the mentality of 'I must follow, even at the expense of the music.' One person *following* another does not have anything to do with music at all; we are musical partners and we have to go *with* each other. Even when what one is playing is not a *duo* sonata, and the piano part is a legitimate 'accompaniment', it still has its own logic of structure, and the pianist has to be allowed to keep the integrity of his part. Every part in every ensemble is at one time or another carrying another part on its shoulders; and each must be able to do this without losing the integrity of his own part. Musicians need to learn to think and behave like equals, and not carry time-worn and artificial rankings out on to the platform and into their music-making.

Fourteen

Some Thoughts on the Performance of Seventeenth- and Eighteenth-century Music

'The Violoncello is an admirable Instrument, whether we consider the sweetness of its Tones, its varied Expression, or its prodigious Compass. In the hands of a Master it yields to no instrument in Solos; and it is indispensably necessary to sustain the Bass in Concerts.'
New Instructions for the Violoncello
(Anon., *c*. 1765)

Playing early music on the modern cello

With all the recent developments in 'authentic' or 'period' instruments and performance in recent years, most cellists are aware of the modifications in string instruments in the nineteenth and twentieth centuries (see also the historical section, pp. 208ff). These changes, principally to the bridge height and fingerboard angle, were essential if the cello was to keep pace, and remain partners with, the ever-increasing sound of the piano; but they also went hand-in-glove with evolving concepts of sound qualities, colours and textures.

Not every cellist today is going to find it possible, or perhaps even desirable, to acquire a second instrument for eighteenth-century playing. But this should not prevent him from playing this early music with a sound and stylistic sense appropriate to its world. We must still be able to live in those worlds of sound and explore their colours and textures within the widened dynamic range of our modern instruments. This means learning to discipline ourselves to the language of a piece despite the range given to us by later developments in our instrument.

The cello has its own nature in relation to the music of the Baroque and Classical eras, and we in the twentieth century too often refuse to concede it that nature. We forget that the cello existed then and that *we* are the latecomers. We do not have to copy the sounds of the Baroque cello exactly, but we need not abuse the emotions or the colours of the music because we know that our modern cello can take us further and can go into all sorts of worlds the Baroque cello never knew (forgetting that the Baroque cellist knew worlds of sound which the modern cellist has not even thought about). We must always keep in mind not only the character of the instrument for which a piece was written, but the fact that most seventeenth- and eighteenth-century composers were also performers, and that their compositions therefore grew out of their first-hand knowledge of the sounds and colours they could produce on their instruments. They did not separate the one thing from the other, and we must not separate them either, for they are one of the roots of the great beauty of this music.

The greatest deficiency in twentieth-century playing is that we have not embraced all the earlier centuries of string playing and incorporated them in our playing. Through over-concentration on recent developments in sound, twentieth-century cellists have actually limited their repertory of sounds. The limitation came when, enamoured with the new sounds which evolving modifications allowed the cello to have, cellists forgot that their instrument was still capable of most of the sound qualities, colours and textures of earlier eras. It was as if a painter, discovering the colour red for the first time, wanted to paint everything in red. Many cellists seemed to believe that the only sound worth hearing on the cello was discovered by the late Romantics – and when they played music of any other period they painted it Romantic 'red' as well. We should, of course, be happy that the set-up on our modern instruments does give them the potential for a bigger, warmer and more open sound – there's nothing wrong with 'red' – but we should like other colours as well. We should want to keep all the great variety of colours and subtle shadings the seventeenth and eighteenth centuries gave us, and add to them our nineteenth- and twentieth-century sounds.

The abuse of the sound of the cello in eighteenth-century music comes about partly because all of us have been brought up with a false impression of what the Baroque and Classical language in music is really like; this false impression often leads us to try to make it 'do' something in terms of our modern concepts. We have been unconsciously led to relate to it in terms of a distorted understanding of its language.

Let me put it this way: supposing I were able overnight to take away all the trees in the world and put artificial ones in their place. And then suppose a child were born into this environment and grew up knowing only artificial trees. He would be bound to accept them, and would probably think that they were very nice because he had been told so, and because he had never seen anything else to compare them with. For him the distortion would be the only reality, and the way he would use trees and relate to them would be in terms of the distortion.

We in the twentieth century suffer from a similar distortion in our concepts of sound, expression and playing techniques *vis-à-vis* the music of the seventeenth and eighteenth centuries – a distortion which began in the late nineteenth century and which so perniciously pervades our concepts of sound creation that many people have come to believe that our modern sound concepts represent an 'advance' over earlier concepts, that composers would have preferred to hear their works performed the way we do now if only they had been given the choice. If this is true, then should not modern artists, by the same token, repaint all the Rembrandts and Turners and Van Goghs in the style of Picasso or Braque? Would Michelangelo not have wished to paint like Picasso if only he had known how?

This eagerness to edit or rearrange music of the past rests on the supposition that Baroque and Classical composers were somehow less capable of expressing emotions and beauty in their music than we are today, and that it is therefore incumbent upon us to 'save' this somewhat incompetent music from oblivion by updating it according to the greater enlightenment of our age. But can we honestly maintain that Boccherini would have preferred this up-dated version of his A major Sonata to the purity of textures, colour and lines he gave it in the original? Consider the first two bars:

If we are willing to accept Baroque and Classical paintings and the poetry of earlier centuries at face value, why do we find it so necessary to tinker around with the music and paint it over with a wash of twentieth-century ideas and concepts?

I personally think that all this up-dating and 'beautifying' came about because people in the latter part of the nineteenth century and the early part of this century were so intent upon their own particular musical language that they were blinded in a way to the great beauty that this earlier music had in its original form. By passing on their blindness through arrangements and editions of this music, they have unwittingly caused generations of musicians to grow up completely unaware of the magnificence of these works in their original form. Were modern cellists to hear some of these works as they were originally intended, they might think they were hearing an incredible bit of magic.

Original instrumentation and modern editions

The great beauty of Baroque and Classical music in the original instrumental combinations is something which only a handful of cellists has recently begun to explore. Most cellists remain ignorant of the fact that the sonatas of Vivaldi, Sammartini, Boccherini and others were intended to be accompanied by a harpsichord and continuo cello, or by a second cello alone. Arranging these works for cello and piano (with the piano part usually written in a florid late-nineteenth-century style) is a distortion so great that it would render them almost unrecognizable to their creators. Their charm and depth of expression are greatly diminished or destroyed entirely by such editing and arrangements, and we are the ones who lose out in the end.

It is not only on matters of instrumentation, but also in the more subtle areas of bowings, phrasings and fingerings that modern editions have led people astray. Whole generations of cellists have known this music only through the distorted view some editors have given them, and have blindly accepted that the editor's rearrangement is *the* composition. No wonder that many cellists have missed their depth of beauty entirely and have used these magnificent works as little show pieces or curtain-raisers in their recitals.

Of course, any work allows for the possibility of some kind of emotion which one can manufacture in relation to it. Even in a modern reworking of a Baroque or Classical sonata the same series of notes is usually left more or less intact in the solo part, and they do move one to a certain extent. But that does not mean that the wonderful original creation is brought back. The same notes dressed in the wrong garb can be at best a bad caricature of something which in its original form was finely wrought and perfectly poised.

Discovery through uncorrupted editions

If we want to discover the original beauty of our early repertoire, we need to go to the original editions of this music. This is not as difficult as one might think, for many libraries throughout Europe and America contain often large amounts of Baroque and Classical cello sonatas and other chamber works in editions dating from the time of composition. In addition, several publishers have in recent years begun to bring out uncorrupted versions of this music, and the serious cellist needs only to do a little judicious shopping.

These original, or later but uncorrupted, editions are valuable because they can lead us to search out alternative possibilities of performance which will bring us closer to that world of musical creation. They provide the kind of healthy soil that one wants to send one's roots into and show us the way back to earlier worlds of expression. Through them one begins to develop a sense of the spirit of this music, and also a sense of the technique one needs in order to portray all its dimensions.

The language of this early music is ultimately tied up with the techniques for creating it: and they, in turn, are closely bound up with uncorrupted editions that do not lead one astray with a welter of bowings and fingerings. This must be the starting point for any cellist who is interested in expanding his musical horizons to these eras of cello performance.

By playing from early or uncorrupted editions, cellists will learn that bowings rarely exist in seventeenth- and eighteenth-century music except as suggestions to the performer, and that fingerings are almost entirely absent. While sparsity of bowing indications does not necessarily mean that everything was played with separate bows, one does discover that separate bows were much more common than we would think today. And from that launching pad one begins to explore and discover the world of variation one can have in separate strokes. Detached bows were part and parcel of the Baroque instrumental style, but it was not just a dull pushing and shoving of down-bows and up-bows: they had a subtlety and variety of articulations within the separate bows that can make our standard twentieth-century bowings seem limited and impoverished by comparison.

Depth of expression in early music

The confusion between depth of feeling and the expression of superficial sensuality is one of the great illnesses of our age. In the seventeenth and eighteenth centuries they had just as much sensuousness and just as much ardour as we have today – in fact, it was even greater, I would say, because it was much less superficial. Read some of the poems of the period, listen to Shakespeare: could one say he is not ardent? Not sensuous? No passion there? He has the whole universe of feeling! These passions are not just a discovery of our time.

Yet so many modern players have been conditioned to think that if they cannot express passion in a way that is (perhaps) appropriate to late-nineteenth- and twentieth-century music, then they must leave it out altogether. This narrow view misses the point completely. Early music has a spiritual hugeness which requires passion and sensuousness for its expression; but at the same time the dimension of the spirit also elevates those qualities into something which goes worlds beyond the purely superficial expression of passion. These qualities are so completely intertwined with one another that if you miss the one, you have lost the other. (Even in later music I sometimes wonder if we do not fail to recognize that which is spiritually very deep because it is often so close to something which is also sensuous that we let ourselves get sucked into that more familiar and therefore easier mainstream.)

It is important to recognize that there is in music a tonal equivalent of feel which can be basically so impure that the sensuousness loses its nobility, and the emotional language, thus abused, is brought to a level dispossessed of dignity. One sidesteps this risk to a greater degree on the Baroque cello because its very nature resists this kind of superficiality, but the modern cello can lend itself to this kind of vulgar sensuality if the player allows himself to be drawn into that world of stereotyped forms of superficial expression. On the modern cello, therefore, it is up to the player to resist this 'pull' and develop instead a sensitivity towards the magnetism of the other musical and spiritual pole. As I said before, this music has a spiritual hugeness, and one can take it much further when one gets into its own language. In the end it can be much more moving when its language is not denied it.

The language of style

A student asked me once, 'How much should I use modern phrasings when I play Baroque music?' This kind of question always makes me wonder what people mean by 'modern' phrasing. If a work has any greatness or validity at all, then it is modern forever on its own terms. How can you have a 'modern' interpretation of an old work (or an 'old' interpretation of a modern work)? Every composition has its own world, and it must become an absolute instinct with performers to recognize it. It is not something you calculate any more than you calculate the recognition of the taste of food: if you put a piece of fish in your mouth, your palate does not react as if it were a piece of melon – it savours it differently because it recognizes the difference of its nature.

Just as a great actor should have the technique and vision to deliver King Lear or Hamlet one night and do a twentieth-century comedy on the next, so musicians should have it as second nature to 'deliver' the music of any composer – to have the pliability of technique and imagination to live within the spirit of many worlds. There is no reason why cellists should not be able to switch from the incredible 'simplicity' of Bach to the emotionally different sphere of Bloch's *Schelomo*. Each has his own world; the greater the spiritual horizon of the composition the greater our instrumental horizon must be.

Think for a minute of the vastness of spirit in the music of Bach, and the range of technical command needed to serve that spirit – and yet how often this vastness is narrowed down because players have confused it with a nineteenth-century Romantic approach (and a limited one at that). Of course, we do not want to hear something like the Dvořák Concerto played as if it were Bach (that would confine it, too, in a different way), but by the same token, we should not hear Bach played like Dvořák. Certainly by the time one is able even to consider playing works like the Dvořák Concerto and the Bach Suites, the mental agility, the sense of style, and the sheer physical control for playing in different 'languages' should come to one so naturally that they are almost instinctive.

You can expand in any language to an endlessness, but it is an endlessness *within the framework of that language*. Things only start to go wrong when you come out of that framework, when you break down the door and go into a room that has a different character and nature. You can break out of the bounds of any era – Modern and Romantic, as well; not doing so is a matter of understanding the completeness of the style and character of a particular music. And it is only this kind of understanding that can guide one to the right sound for a particular era of music – whether one plays on 'modern' or 'authentic' instruments.

Part Two

The Basics of Technique on the Cello

We must never lose sight of the basics of technique, for they provide the foundations upon which all else is built; but we must also know how to use all the music we play to stretch those foundations until they are opened up to encompass the endless demands of the music.

One
Holding the Cello

An eighteenth-century tutor describes the correct holding position for the cello as follows: 'To hold this Instrument commodiously for performing, rest the Body of it between the calves of your Legs, the edge of the Back on the left Leg, the edge of the Belly on the right. For this purpose it is necessary that the right Leg be placed perpendicularly on the ground, and the left so extended that its foot may extend four or five inches beyond the other.'

Although the author is describing the position for what we today would call a 'Baroque cello' and assumes that there is no endpin to support the instrument (see below, page 263–4), the position he has set forth is still basically correct for the modern cello. The position of the modern cello, with its spike, is really a variation on this theme. The only minor difference is that the use of the spike allows us to place the left knee slightly more behind the cello, thus giving greater clearance on the A string.

Angle of the cello when playing

Though one always wants a certain degree of flexibility in the angle of the cello while playing, I personally find it advantageous to play with the cello basically turned slightly towards the right so that the strings can meet the bow more directly. The 'square' position of the cello, shown in the second of the photographs opposite, seems to me to be slightly disadvantageous because the angle of the bow to the strings is already less direct. A cello which is turned to the left, as shown in the lower picture, is extremely

Turned slightly to
the right (strings
turned to meet bow)

'Square'

Turned to the left
(strings turned away
from bow)

awkward. This position turns the strings *away* from the
bow and forces the right arm into an awkward position as
it chases after them. It also forces the left shoulder back,
upsetting the whole equilibrium of the body and diminishing the effectiveness of sound production.

Many cellists, in spite of the support which the spike
gives, try to grip the cello in an inflexible position, using

the knees to hold it like a vice. Yet even the Baroque cello was never 'gripped' with the legs: on the contrary, the Baroque hold was one of the most relaxed imaginable. With the cello cradled on the lower part of the calves, supporting it was as easy as dropping something into a basket. But one sees *modern* cellists, who should have even greater freedom of their legs because they do not even have to make a 'basket' to cradle the cello in, gripping with their knees as if they thought they were trying to ride a wild horse bareback. Not only is this unnecessary, but the tension thus created in the legs spreads upwards and causes tension in the muscles of the upper body.

The backward slope of the cello

The natural use of the body in relation to the instrument is something to which all cellists should give thought. The slightly greater backward slant that the end-pin allows in holding the cello should never be exaggerated to the point where it contradicts one's feeling of embracing the cello: one wants to lean *forward* to meet and embrace the cello, not retreat *backwards* away from it.

The use of an over-long end-pin can force the cellist into a position which is both physically and psychologically contradictory to his playing. We have already talked about the physical contradiction: the absurdity of trying to embrace something and pull away from it at the same time. The psychological contradiction comes from the effect of body position on one's concentration and involvement. Normally a person who is intent upon what he is doing and upon his actions or communication will lean forward. It is an instinctive position which most people will be able to observe in themselves in many situations. For a cellist to lean backwards in an almost slouching position, when he should be intent upon what he is doing and actively engaged in the communication of musical ideas, cannot but undermine both his attentiveness and the power of his communication.

I know that the arguments for the longer end-pin centre around the use of the natural pull of gravity to gain more power with the bow. But ask those same people who put forth this argument to open a jar when the lid has stuck and you will see them instinctively bring it into their midriff for the extra power they need. The fact is that the natural power of the arm muscles when they pull something in towards the body is far greater than the pull of gravity: we could actually crush our cellos in our embrace if we wanted to – we have easily more power than the instrument can possibly take. That is why I advocate holding the cello as if to embrace it. You will find that you not only have more power, but that the use of your body in relation to the instrument will be more natural.

There are of course certain individuals who, because of abnormal height or arm length, will need the longer spike in order to establish a position at the cello which is roughly commensurate with that of other cellists. It is not the use of the long end-pin, but the *indiscriminate* use of it that I find troubling. The length of the end-pin must relate very much to the needs of the individual cellist, and for the person of average build the over-long end-pin only creates an abnormal and, as we have seen, contradictory use of the body *vis-à-vis* the instrument.

Two
Bow Command

Because it is the right hand which must open the expressive doors for the left, it is important for cellists to learn from the start to create their sound from their right hand, and to *know* that it is the right hand that is creating the sound.

Learning to hold the bow (Baroque hold)

I think it is valuable to begin playing the cello with a Baroque bow hold (i.e., holding the bow loosely in the hand more toward the centre of the stick as illustrated opposite). It alleviates the awkwardness that nearly everyone feels at the beginning and also sidesteps the unnatural compensations one is inclined to make to relieve the feeling of awkwardness. (This is particularly true for children, whose muscles are less developed.) A modified version of the 'Baroque hold' can be achieved on any modern bow by simply holding the bow a few inches closer towards the middle of the stick. The hand in this hold is so beautifully positioned on the stick that it creates a perfectly balanced weight throughout the length of the bow during the life of the stroke. This position also encourages a continuity of flow in the arm movement so that the whole note, on either upbow or downbow, becomes a living substance.

Through the establishment of this hold, the beginner will find it easier to retain the same feel in his hand and arm, and the same quality of sound, as he moves back into the modern hold. Once the feel for the continuity of stroke has been established, the student will more easily be able to counteract the unevenness of use – of contact with the

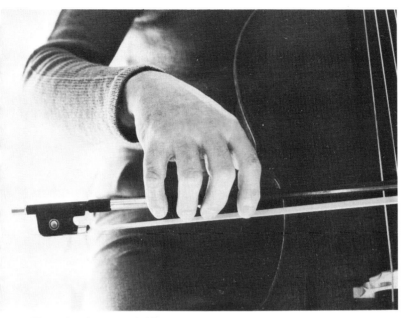

The modified 'Baroque hold'

string, and of attack in the various parts of the bow – inherent in the modern bow, and will be able to use the modern bow with more discretion and with greater command of sound.

All cellists, however advanced, should occasionally play with the Baroque hold on the modern bow as a reminder both of the sound and of the feel in the hand and arm; it is always useful to rediscover periodically the beautiful, unhampered continuity of flow of arm and sound which is the very nature of this hold and stroke. The modern bow makes different demands upon the player because it responds to the demands of later music, and to meet these the cellist has to develop the facility of different techniques which the different parts of the modern bow require (for an elaboration of these techniques, please see Part One, Chapter 6, 'The Craft of the Bow'). But he should never lose sight of the fact that in later music there are many notes which aspire to the great purity of sound and perfection of action which the Baroque hold can inspire and develop.

Basic bow arm position and movement

The continuity of the flow of movement through the bow as we travel from one end to the other will establish the relationship and interplay between the muscles and joints of the upper and lower arm, the wrist and the fingers. If we stiffen a joint at any point along this flow of movement, we shall throw the entire mechanism out. This is why a released flexibility of muscles and joints, allowing a natural play of motion from one part off the other, is essential to good bow movement and hence sound.

As you can see from the illustrations opposite, there is at all points a free line from the elbow through the wrist and hand. When the bow is at the frog, the wrist may be slightly convex (depending on the body build of the cellist), but it should never be humped, or the line to the elbow will be destroyed (see the pictures on p. 154). As one begins to draw the bow, the elbow will move away from the body until about mid-point in the bow. Then the flow of the movement is continued as the elbow, serving as a loose hinge, opens out to let the forearm continue the stroke the upper arm has begun. At all times the wrist remains in a free line with the elbow (though it may, when you reach the point, become slightly concave).

Because every human being is unique, the precise way in which a cellist achieves these basic guidelines will be something he has to work out on his own or with his teacher. The important thing is that one should understand the nature of the movements one makes with the arm, wrist and hand in bowing – and the naturalness of unfettered, logical movement – and let that govern one's use of the body in bowing.

Positions of elbow and wrist in bowing

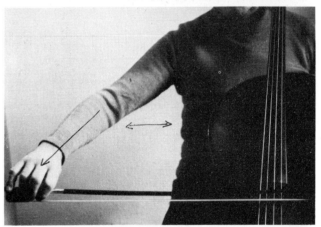

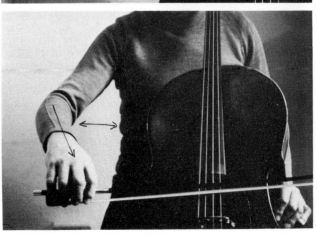

Straight line from elbow to wrist

Curved line from elbow to wrist (weaker)

The position of the thumb in holding the bow

The position of the thumb against the stick creates one of the greatest problems for cellists. There is no single solution because there are so many different hand structures. Some people have short thumbs, others long; some have weak joints, others stiff joints; some are double-jointed; and so on. Ultimately one cannot hope to pin down the problem in words in a way that will solve every cellist's problem; that is something the teacher has to explore with the pupil, or the cellist with himself alone.

One of the best ways of searching for solutions to thumb problems can come through holding the bow with the thumb *beneath* the frog, as illustrated on pp. 155–6.

154

Although this hold was fairly common in the eighteenth century as a real playing position, I would not recommend its use for modern playing but suggest it purely as an investigation into the relationship of the thumb and fingers in the bow hold (it is easier for the thumb to relate itself naturally *vis-à-vis* the other fingers within the larger circle of the frog *plus* the stick than on the narrowness of the stick alone). As an experiment it is quite useful because it stabilizes the hand on the bow and gives one a bearing on what may be needed to correct problems (particularly when a cellist is wrestling with a problem thumb). By allowing him to come at his problems from a different angle, it often gives fresh insight into their solution.

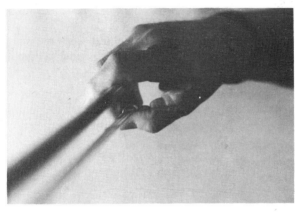

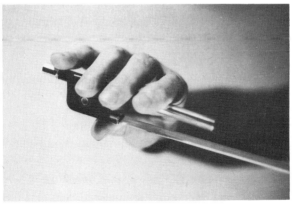

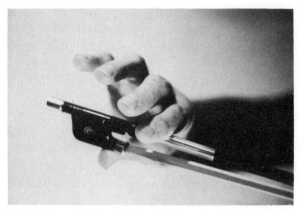

Holding bow with thumb beneath the frog

Relationship of the thumb to the other fingers

What one will derive from the above experiment is the knowledge that in holding the modern bow in the normal position, one must not let the thumb be square in relation to the other fingers. When you make a fist, you can see what the natural angle of the thumb is to the rest of the hand: the thumb does not squarely oppose the fingers, but comes towards them from an angle. This relationship is the cornerstone of a natural bow hold. From the series of photographs opposite it is easy to see the nature of the thumb–fingers relationship and how the bow hold (particularly the use of the thumb in the bow hold) grows out of the naturalness of the closed fist.

It is the *corner* of the thumb that should sit against the stick, and it fits most easily into the niche which occurs where the front of the frog meets the stick. By fitting the thumb into that little corner, you will not only have a comfortable and natural position for it, but one that encourages correct placing (see top of p. 158).

The forefinger

The forefinger is all-important in terms of bow-string contact and bow articulations, and it is essential that cellists should develop from the start a proper regard for the use of this finger. The position of the forefinger, and the relative placement of the other fingers, is illustrated on p. 158. To understand the proper working relationship between the fingers, the reader is referred to Part One, Chapter 6, 'The Craft of the Bow'.

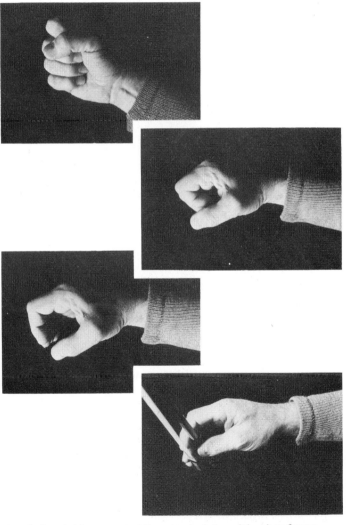

How the bow hold grows out of the natural relation of thumb to fingers

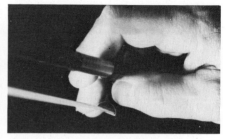

Correct placing of thumb

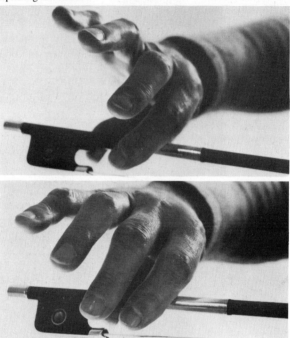

Use of the forefinger alone as a means of investigating
its importance in sound creation

Normal hand position showing relative
placement of fingers on the stick

Three
The Playing Position of the Left Hand

The slope of the left hand determines the angle at which the fingers meet the strings. It also governs the degree of independence the fingers are going to have and hence their capacity to discriminate in minute pitch differences.

The 'square' hand is often praised as a good cello hand, but when the hand is held 'square' to the cello (the 'squareness' of the hand usually being determined by the angle of the two middle fingers to the string), the first and fourth fingers are forced into positions which are anything but 'square' and which also severely limit their freedom and agility. The fourth finger especially is handicapped by this position. When the two middle fingers are 'square' to the string, it is all but impossible not to deform the fourth finger: it meets the string at an angle like an old shoe which is worn down at the side. (See illustrations on page 160)

Now look at the lower pictures, where the hand is shown in a 'sloped' position. The differences in the various finger lengths have been evened up and each finger is given an equal degree of independence, and thus discrimination in pitch differentiation; and the fourth finger does not have to become bandy-legged in order to reach the fingerboard. (Incidentally, if you turn the bottom right-hand picture around, as on p. 161, you will discover that this position is very similar to the left-hand position of the violinist!)

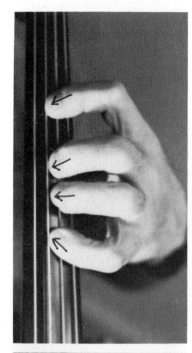

Angle of fingers
with 'square' hand

Angle of fingers with the hand
in a sloped position

Similarity to left-hand position of violinist

The sloped position of the left hand has a great bearing on many factors. Because there is a straight line from the hand back to the elbow the hand is centralized, and this not only allows a free and direct transmission of the energy of the hand into the string (giving the sound greater richness and expression) but also enables the hand to create a vibrato which has perfect movement to either side of the point of contact (and hence a core which can be expanded or contracted at will).

It is important to stress, however, that one needs to discover the right degree of slope for each individual hand. My hand is not someone else's hand. The sloped position illustrated is only a *basic* position. All hand shapes are different and all finger lengths are different, and therefore the slope will vary slightly from person to person. This is again something which needs investigation on the part of both the teacher and the student.

The difficulties engendered by the set hand

One is usually taught as a general principle when learning the cello to hold the fingers down. While this practice has its place in teaching beginners so that they learn the feel of hand position and develop a rough idea of the relative spacing of the notes under the fingers, teachers too often forget to tell students when to *stop* holding their fingers down.

One should actually teach both uses of the hand at the same time, encouraging the student to combine a knowledge of holding his fingers down with the ability to release them. A more flexible approach will give him knowledge of relative note position without causing him to lose his feel for flexibility in the hand, but if it is not taught from the start, the clamped position will become such a habit that when the student tries to switch over to the released hand he will find it very difficult.

One of the great disadvantages of the set hand with all the fingers clamped down is that it destroys the natural flexibility within the hand. And this in turn renders impossible any attempt at fine tuning, for once the hand is set in a fixed position it will lose the ability of independent redistribution of weight and finger position which is essential for fine tuning. (This is a subject about which we have talked at length in Part One.)

Another disadvantage of playing with the fingers held down is that it makes a free vibrato difficult, if not impossible. Trying to vibrate with the fingers held down is like trying to rock a flat-bottomed boat – an absolute contradiction in logic. Even if one manages to eke out a kind of vibrato under those circumstances, it will lack all possibility of subtlety in its use because the control of the degrees with which one uses it is so severely limited from the start.

It is *independence* of the fingers, very much in a pianistic sense, that we want. However, independence of the fingers does not mean that the fingers one is not using are sticking up in the air. Even if one consciously lifts the fingers as an antidote to the habit of holding them down, one should always remember that 'lift' does not necessarily mean 'height'. There are degrees of height – the lower fingers might even rest gently on the string, or feather it when the upper fingers are playing – and it is as counter-productive to stiffen the hand in order to keep the fingers off the strings as it is to try to hold them all down.

The important point, as shown by the pictures below, is that the fingers that are not being used in playing should be released, that the life should flow into the one finger as it flows out of the previous finger – *because* it flows out of the previous finger (like the way we use our legs when we walk). There is a world of difference in the feel and

'Release' and independence of fingers

effectiveness of the hand when it is used this way – and there is also a world of difference in the sound and in the expressive potential of the left hand.

The set hand with fingers held down also greatly increases the difficulty of shifting. By multiplying the amount of friction between the fingers and the string (through more fingers being pressed against the string), this use of the hand increases the amount of energy needed to move from one place on the fingerboard to another.

One sees this at its worst in shifts in the thumb position when a cellist clamps all his fingers tightly to the string and then strains to move this whole apparatus up and down the fingerboard. How much easier all his shifts become when only the fingers actually engaged in playing maintain contact with the string. And how much easier it is to make light, delicate shifts as well as fast, forceful ones.

Playing with one finger (just as an exercise) is a good way of combating a set hand while practising shifting at the same time. I remember a cellist coming to one of my master classes some years ago and starting to play the Elgar Concerto with the most tightly locked hand imaginable. What came out of that rigid hand was impossible to describe. So I asked him to play the whole tune again, but this time on one finger – and the transformation was amazing. It was by no means a finished performance, but because he was forced to let go and release his hand even slightly, already much of what was wrong in his playing had disappeared. I would urge any student who wants to combat a set hand (or any teacher who wants to help his pupils combat set hands) to begin by playing scales on one finger (let each finger in turn have a go at it) just to see what it teaches him about hand tension and release.

The myth of the 'weak fourth finger'

When cellists complain that their fourth finger is weak, I find that there are usually several ways of assessing their problem. If, for instance, they have been in the habit of playing with a 'square' hand, then the reduced mobility of the fourth finger could indeed make it feel weaker. Or their fourth finger may actually be weak if they have been used to playing with their fingers held down and never given it a chance to develop as the other fingers have. Imagine what our first fingers would be like, even assuming that they are stronger to start out with, if it were the other way around and they were always made to play with the support of the other fingers. A crutch only maintains weakness in a limb, and a finger which is never allowed to play on its own is bound not only to feel weak but, in time, actually to become weaker than its neighbours.

But the most pervasive reason for cellists feeling that their fourth fingers are weak comes, I think, from a misleading measurement of the *relative* strength and use of the fingers. If the measurement of strength in the fingers is based upon the maximum power of each finger, then the fourth finger will seem relatively weaker. But the question that is never asked is whether one needs the full power of the first and second fingers. A finger may be weaker in relation to the other fingers and still have all the strength it needs to do the job it has to do. I suspect that people's thinking about this tends to go wrong when they focus on the physical action alone, instead of on what has to be achieved by that physical action.

I would suggest that one develop instead the ability to relate the action to the desired end result. Your fingers have different weights and different powers, and therefore they need to be used differently, and with discrimination, to achieve an equal end. It is the equal use of the unequal weights and powers of the fingers (through an unvaried hammer action used to a maximum, irrespective of the differences in the fingers) that causes things to go wrong, and misleads people into assuming a weak fourth finger.

Hammered fingers and subtlety of 'tread'

Hammered fingers are doubly deadly because they also

prevent the development of any sensitivity of 'tread'. (By 'tread' I am referring to the ways in which the finger can put itself down on the string.) Consider the way a good pianist runs up and down the keyboard at every dynamic level, using every finger, and still is able to give every note the same attack and evenness of sound, or shade the notes according to the musical requirements. If pianists were to hammer their fingers, each to its maximum capacity, then every single note in their runs would stick out with a different dynamic! Cellists get by with this kind of illogical use of their fingers because it is not the fingers but the bow which actually creates the sound on the cello (though they often forget that). The way in which the fingers of the left hand contribute to that sound will be greatly undermined if they are allowed to hammer each note with maximum power and no consideration of sensitivity or 'tread'.

Playing with hammered fingers not only defeats sensitivity of tread, but at the same time serves to strengthen the myth of the weak fourth finger. If, when a young cellist is developing the muscles in his fingers and learning control, his striving for power if allowed to go on in one direction only, and he is not encouraged to assess and understand the diversity of powers his fingers have, then he is not only likely to become insensitive to the variety of finger treads possible to him, but he is probably also going to complain that his fourth finger is 'weak'. Developing cellists should never be allowed (much less encouraged) to use their fingers in a single hammered action, but should be schooled to understand the many grades of power, the many *variations* of power the fingers possess. The compulsion to play with maximum finger attack all the time is actually a sign of weak and undisciplined fingers. Strength also lies in delicacy – and in all the degrees between the extremes of power. Instead of using x pounds pressure on all fingers, they should learn to assess the relative strength of each finger against the requirement of stopping the string and accept that as the starting point. From there they can develop an infinite variety of tread, and the fourth finger will take its rightful place as a member of the team.

Over-gripping with the left hand

The fingers, to have free and independent movement, have to be able to have a healthy uplift as well as a down-drop; in fact the freedom of the uplift action is almost more important than the down-drop. (It is the same principle we use when we walk or run: how can you begin to take a step if you do not first *lift* the leg you intend to take the next step on?)

Try grasping anything – a bottle, a glass – and you will see how naturally the fingers and thumb oppose each other. You will also see how impossible it is for the thumb to exert more pressure than the fingers, or the fingers to exert more pressure than the thumb – you cannot press one harder than the other. It is a natural pincer movement where the force of the one side is always met by an equal force from the other.

When the thumb is squeezed tightly against the neck of the cello, it entices the fingers to oppose it with an equal pressure – thus the attempt to release a finger, as it prepares for a downstroke, actually becomes an unbalancing factor. Because the pressure of the thumb dictates that the finger meet it with an equal pressure, the lift of the finger becomes a contradiction in physical logic; since the finger cannot back away from the pressure of the thumb, any attempt to force it to do so is made an awkward and unnatural movement.

Now, as it happens, the most convenient position for the thumb when one is playing in the lower positions is behind the neck and opposite the fingers. But we must not let the similarity of this position to a 'holding' position trap us into using the thumb and fingers in a pincer movement. The thumb has to have great fluidity and a vast variety of pressures as it moves in a relaxed way with the hand, moving even slightly with each finger tread to meet the opposing finger. Cellists need to think very much of the finger articulation of pianists for whom the thumb, when not in use, moves gently with the rest of the hand.

Extended positions

The idea of stretching out to extended position should not cause us to allow tension to come into the hand (the idea of steeling oneself for a stretch is itself a guaranteed muscle shrinker). The hand should move as easily and effortlessly as the opening out of a fan. The logic of the fan works both ways: one can fan out upwards or backwards – both are beautiful in their ease of movement.

This concept is especially useful in thumb position and in the fifth, sixth and seventh positions when one allows the thumb to remain behind on the neck. One should be able to move the hand away from the thumb and back towards it again with the greatest ease, simply letting the circle between the thumb and the rest of the hand enlarge and then come back again. Using the hand this way in thumb position will also help combat the set 'thumb

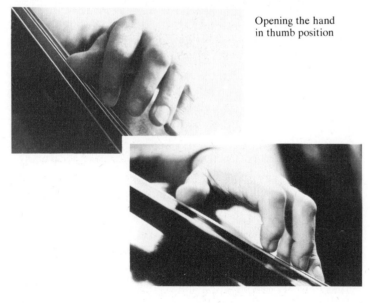

Opening the hand
in thumb position

position hand', which is such an enemy of agility. One has great reach between the thumb and the other fingers and it serves óne well, especially in the high, fast passages where one needs great agility (see the sequences of pictures on pp. 168–9.

Learning the map of the fingerboard

One of the commonest failings in cellists at all levels of playing is that they do not know the map of the fingerboard. They play by rote, putting fingers down on different notes because (if it is a scale) they were taught that fingering, or because it is the fingering marked in the exercise or piece – *but without even knowing what note they are playing.* And if they take a wrong turning with their fingering, they

Opening the hand with the thumb behind the neck

become hopelessly stuck. It is really like 'painting by numbers' on the cello. (Cellists are, I fear, the worst amongst instrumentalists in this. One only has to compare printed editions of cello music with those for violin or piano to see how much more heavily fingered they are – and many cellists fill in the gaps completely by pencilling in the missing fingerings!)

From the start cellists should explore the fingerboard in a way that makes them thoroughly conversant with the location of every note and the many different pathways by which that note can be reached. Just as London taxi drivers are required to take a 'knowledge of London' test to show that they are thoroughly familiar with not just the main thoroughfares but also the many little by-ways and short cuts before they are licensed to drive a cab, so cellists should develop a similarly thorough knowledge of all the notes on their instrument, their alternative positions and the many ways there are of playing almost any passage.

Of course set fingerings are an essential part of one's earliest studies on the cello in order that one can develop a basic knowledge of the lay-out of the notes on the fingerboard, but quite early in their studies pupils should be encouraged to seek out alternative fingerings for their scales and pieces. Orthodox fingerings are only a point of departure. One of the first ways of branching out, even in the earliest stages of playing, can be by playing one-octave scales on a single string (C major on the C string, G major on the G, etc.). This kind of practice helps to develop an awareness that there is more than one place in which the same note can be played on the cello (and provides a familiarity with the higher positions).

Students should also learn to play every scale using only one finger. By doing this they will develop a feel for the distance of an interval and will free themselves from the straitjacket of set fingerings. By experiencing the freedom of mobility in the hand right from the start they will also more easily sidestep the pitfalls of the set-hand position and over-gripping. One can play these scales with each of the four fingers singly (i.e. 1–1–1–1, 2–2–2–2, etc.) and then begin working out various combinations of two, three and eventually four fingers. This kind of practice teaches one both discipline and a free play of the hand at the same time.

Practising scales this way will also make agility and flexibility of fingering seem natural and easy. The student will be able to transfer this mentality of alternative fingerings to his studies and pieces, and, as he learns to search out various fingering possibilities, will gradually build up a body of knowledge of how fingerings relate to colour, texture, phrasing, line. This will enable him eventually to choose fingerings on musical grounds alone.

Even very early in his studies a cellist should be encouraged to find several fingerings for the pieces he plays. A simple work like Hindemith's *Three Easy Pieces* (which are, incidentally, good enough musically for any cellist to play on the concert platform) can be learned at first in the first and half positions, as Hindemith intended; then, once the student has mastered this, with other fingerings which go up into the higher positions and which also fulfil the music.

The more a cellist experiments with various fingerings in anything he plays, the more knowledgeable he will become of the map of the fingerboard. He will discover that the same finger sequence set in a different musical and emotional context will not feel the same, and he will begin to develop such a tremendous agility of fingering that he can almost hear in advance what a particular fingering is going to do to the musical content of a passage.

Part Three

Teachers and Parents

Music is a vast mansion – and all of its many rooms have to be furnished by the student as he grows into a musician. Yet most students, even those near the end of their studies, approach their task as if they were going to furnish a bedsitter. They have no idea of the dimensions. Whether this comes from the teacher or the student, I cannot say.

One
Attitudes towards Teaching

If the teacher cannot find a solution relative to the talent and temperament of any one pupil, then it is he, not the pupil, who has failed.

One of the greatest failings in teaching can be a lack of understanding of the need for the spiritual and emotional alignment between the teacher and the pupil. When you undertake to work with a pupil, you must first harness his heart and mind to your heart and mind, for without that close link you cannot really teach him. At the same time, however, you have to be able to stand back from him so that he does not become submerged in your personality, but will be encouraged to grow and blossom into whatever his potentials and inclinations will allow him to become. A respect on the part of the teacher for the unique nature and temperament of each pupil is also essential. Students should never be approached as if they were made of one substance. It is the role of the teacher rather to encourage them to discover themselves, and it should be within the power of the teacher to develop each pupil's musical personality in terms of what it *is*, not in terms of some abstract or formulated 'norm'.

Each pupil is for the teacher a path for further exploration and expansion of his own knowledge, each untrodden path a pushing back of the boundaries of his old self, each new situation leading to an endless universe of knowledge and understanding. Ultimately, the teacher must be able to contain within himself all the many 'selves' that come to him to study. By approaching teaching in this way the teacher will be able to enlarge his own musical horizons and his whole experience of teaching through the problems brought to him by individual pupils.

Just as there are no two fingerprints alike, there are no two personalities and talents alike, and each pupil has to be nurtured according to his temperament and talent. Even the same student is never twice the same: apart from dispositional differences from day to day, he is also evolving as a person, in the mastery of his instrument, and in the maturing of his understanding of musical matters.

It is really very short-sighted (even in a purely selfish sense) for teachers to take pride in developing their pupils into replicas of themselves: the same style, the same phrasings, the same bowings, fingerings, mannerisms, whims – even the same mistakes! And it is defeating for both sides if the teacher's satisfaction in his pupil's progress is measured entirely by the degree to which the student is getting to sound like him (this is a misleading measure of progress, anyway, if the word is to be understood in its widest sense).

This is why I find it so wrong for a teacher to dismiss a pupil's way of doing something merely on the grounds that it is not the way he, the teacher, does it. The teacher has to know how to step outside his own personality and get inside that of his pupil; he has to be able to feel what he feels and think what he thinks. Then he can step back again and be in a better position to help the student unravel his problems. Even when the teacher is able to see the germ of something musically and/or technically wrong in what the pupil is doing, he should have the imagination (and not be so full of his own way) to see even further than the student can into what he is trying to accomplish and help him bring it to its own fulfilment. *Then* he can discuss alternative ways with him and point out what he feels to be the musical errors or technical pitfalls in what the student has just done. But if he wants to prove to the student that his way of doing something is wrong, he can only make his point by comparing the pupil's *fulfilled* idea with his own. (It not only puts the pupil at an unfair disadvantage if the teacher does not first allow him to fulfil his own intent as well as he can before the teacher presents alternative possibilities to him, but it also squashes the development of the student's imagination and leaves him ill-equipped to work on his own when the time comes.)

Why should a teacher *want* to create a secondhand version of himself? The pupil may have something in his own right which, when fully grown, is something no one else has. Why should he not be allowed to express something beautiful differently? Why should he not be *encouraged* to do so? The task of the teacher is not to limit the student to the teacher's musical boundaries, or to stamp him into a mould; the teacher is there to bring out the pupil and help him to discover qualities within himself he never knew he had.

Proper teaching is teaching wisdom. The student must learn how to look at himself; to develop the craft of investigation into his own problems. The teacher should be showing his students the inner secrets of how to cope with themselves, how to listen and correct (and to discover what subtle means of correction they can evolve), to conceptualize and to discriminate – not just carry out orders.

In the process of working out problems, the teacher must be careful that the student is led to a proper sense of balance in assessing himself. To develop this sense of balance he must be encouraged to consider the *good* qualities in his playing as well as the bad. If the student is asked to focus his attention only on the bad and never on the good, and never has it pointed out to him *why* the good is good, how can he develop a sense of balance *vis-à-vis* his own playing and progess? He should, instead, be encouraged to enlarge his technique out of the good things he already does.

By guiding the pupil to work in this way in his own practising and playing, by teaching him to build upon the good, and to break down the various strands of his problems and unravel them one by one, the teacher will develop in him the ability to bring his own powers as a musician to their fullest bloom. At the same time, through self-investigation and the unravelling and breaking down of his own problems, the student will be developing the techniques for teaching others later on (if he should ever decide to teach).

Ultimately, the pupil should be encouraged to view his lesson room as a workroom: he is learning, and this is where to make mistakes and work out answers. The teacher, without losing authority, can convey to the student the feeling that he is a young colleague and that together they are working out the solutions to problems. It follows, therefore, that the teacher should *discuss*, not dictate, fingerings and bowings. There is more than one good fingering for almost any passage, and the student should be made aware of the various possibilities and be led to understand the reasons underlying them. At any level, he will only grow and expand if the teacher leads him to wider vistas in playing.

Two
Developing Naturalness from the Start

Nothing is easier – or more difficult – than playing the cello.

When you start a child on the cello, your first aim should be to gain knowledge and insight into his temperament – his humour, brightness, imagination, sharpness of ear, natural rhythmic sense – before you ever begin to launch into the ABC of the physical act of playing. From there you can begin to stimulate his interest in the instrument *per se*. (While what I say in this chapter is geared to teaching young children, the principles would be the same for beginners of any age, though the methods, which are up to the imagination of the individual teacher anyway, would differ.)

I think the important thing is to captivate and tantalize the child's imagination, really tickle his fantasy. I would begin with the instrument itself, explaining it to the child as if it were a toy and showing him what he can do with it. I would get him really fascinated in the article: what it is made of, how it is made, what makes it sound, what makes things vibrate and what 'vibration' is to 'sound'. I would want to conjure up a real vision about this instrument, because the instrument and the child are going to hold hands, they are going to do things to one another.

It is not enough just to hand him the instrument and tell him the names of the strings, and that he must sit in this way, and hold the bow in that way, and place his fingers on the strings in these places. Let the fascination draw him from the start. It will take him a long way towards discovering the means, and towards having the patience to develop those means.

Then let him pluck the strings and help him draw the bow. Fascinate him with the many sounds that can be made with the bow. The better the foundation for sound is in the right hand, the fewer problems there will be when he puts his left hand with it later on. With the bow he can learn to play little rhythms, fascinating rhythms – children are so receptive to that sort of thing and rather marvellous at it.

When you eventually begin with the left hand, encourage him to explore the entire fingerboard by letting him glide his fingers up and down each string to get the feel for how movement of the left hand changes the pitch. This is a fantasy tickler for the beginner which will make the more disciplined study later on less forbidding, for he will already begin to see the wider context, and he will later understand the purpose of discipline as a means of arriving at a freer and more complete use of the cello – bribery without corruption!

After that he can begin to learn left-hand position, and where the fingers have to be to lie over the basic pitches. Take your cello and play lazy little tunes for him, quite slow ones, and then let him learn to move his hand and fingers to make the same notes (he should try it both ways: playing the tune with just one finger, and then using different fingers). Even at this most basic stage, everything he does on the cello must fascinate the child. Technical study which has no musical counterpart, no place for the imagination, will only become a bore to him.

It is important that the naturalness in any child is developed from the start, and it is up to the teacher to make the child's feeling for naturalness so strong that whenever he becomes unnatural in his movements on the cello, he will begin to feel uncomfortable. Through the habit of naturalness he should become so at home in his use of 'mechanism' that even when things do not work right for him, he will not tense up and use himself wrongly on the cello.

Admittedly, it is an odd sort of 'brain-washing' to give a child, but it is a healthy sort – and through it he will learn to keep a balance in what he does on the cello and in life. Heaven knows that when he becomes an adult many things are going to fight against that naturalness; the more he can learn to keep his uninhibited naturalness as a child, the less chance there is that the fears adulthood can bring with it will be an influencing factor on the way he uses himself. What one is trying to do is implant a correct attitude towards life. I have always maintained that life is therapy for playing the cello, and playing the cello is therapy for life.

Self-built (or teacher-taught) obstacles to playing

I often say that playing the cello is easy, but I say it a bit tongue-in-cheek because I *do* know the difficulties. The point I am trying to make is that people usually start out by making it far more difficult than it is. If everything is natural and healthy on the cello to start with, one will be rid of most of the unnecessary problems and find one's energies freed to tackle the genuine problems.

Most difficulties on the cello are mole-hills made into mountains because people do things which are anti-natural and thereby build prison bars for themselves. If one can destroy those barriers, or better still, never let them develop, then learning the craft of playing is basically much easier. It is up to the teacher to see to it that pupils are not reduced to playing with only half their powers because the other half are busy climbing over obstacles that did not really exist in the first place, obstacles which they have put there themselves out of fear, or through the mishandling of themselves on the instrument.

The tendency to create obstacles is often the result of the pupil's thinking (or being led to think) that he has been given a terribly difficult craft to master. It is true, of course, in a way. But his expressive powers should not be shunted off because he has been shown the one path only; the teacher must not allow the craft aspect of playing to become such a narrow isolated path for the pupil that he cannot let it run parallel to the other path of his musical intentions.

Children are usually able to handle this double aspect of playing beautifully; often they can respond to the parallel paths even better and with greater variety than adults. Certainly it will fascinate the child more if the teacher couples the musical aspect of playing, the fantasy side, with the learning of the physical action that makes it happen on the cello. Fantasy goes hand-in-glove with movement, and movement is one of the commanding aspects of technique.

Three
Teaching the Basics of Technique

I am always perplexed when I hear people say of a teacher, 'Ah, he teaches technique,' or 'You can spot his pupils every time – musically they are terrible, but he *does* teach technique!' How on earth do you teach technique in isolation from that which the technique is applied to? Imagine Rembrandt painting a great picture on technique only! There has to be something else, something for the technique to ride on. If you listen to those pupils, you will soon discover that not only is the musical side of their playing starved, but their technique *per se* is also a very limited and unevenly developed thing. How can one talk about giving pupils '*a* technique'? Every person is going to have a different technique, unique to his own being. All the teacher can give someone is the biggest technique he can have within his means and relative to his growth *vis-à-vis* the music. Technique is not something you can measure with a tape measure. If you have ten different people, you will have ten different techniques.

Even in the earliest stages the teacher must encourage the child to become aware of the sound sensation created by his physical action on the cello, the possibility of mood behind the notes he is playing. That should be there as a germ for a way of life, for a linking of one's expressive nature in a natural and uninhibited way to the physical means for realizing it. It is so misleading when people make a science of being unnatural, and allow the dream/imagination to shrink into oblivion by the physical/mechanical take-over. Of course we can teach the isolated movement, but it will not lead to anything; musically it is still-born. In the end, we have to accept the fact that one cannot teach complete technique, one can only teach the *basics* of technique. From there it is the music (under the teacher's guidance) that teaches unending technique.

Most of the basics of technique were covered in earlier chapters. However, there are certain basics, and aspects of basics, which I have saved for this chapter because they are so closely linked up with the teacher: these have mainly to do with those aspects of bow technique and left-hand technique which are best learned by getting the 'feel' of a basic movement through the guiding hand of a good teacher.

Playing with a straight bow

It is a near impossibility for someone during his first lessons on the cello even to begin to feel what a straight line in bowing is. Therefore it becomes all-important in the early stages of bowing that the teacher be vigilant in guiding the student towards a fusion of the feel in his right hand and arm when the bow is straight with overt knowledge of its straightness. The teacher can help instil this feeling in the pupil in lessons, but when the pupil is on his own he should be encouraged to practise in front of a mirror so that he can develop a realistic understanding of where and how the bow is sitting on the string. (The view he has from 'above' – when he looks down from a playing position – gives him a distorted picture which he eventually has to put in a correct perspective.)

By this kind of early training the student will be able to establish a feel for the bow sitting in an imaginary 'groove' on the string and will quickly make corrections if the bow starts to slip sideways or move diagonally. In time, the feel in the hand and arm for this 'groove' will become supported by a concomitant 'feel' in the ear for the sound of the bow when it has established correct contact with the string.

The more ingrained this kind of practice becomes in the early stages, the less likely that the healthy functioning of the bow will be interfered with by the early stages of left-hand action. There is always a tendency, when the two are brought together for the first time, for the activities of the left hand to distract the concentration in the right, but the stronger the mechanism of the right is (both in terms of feel in the arm and hand, and in terms of 'feel' in the ear), the more easily it will resist this distraction. The greater the strength of a mechanism, the greater its defence against confusion.

The many grooves of texture

The teacher must quite early on make the child aware of the many different sounds he can create by using the different areas of the strings between the fingerboard and bridge. He can sow the seed for this awareness by drawing the bow with his hand over the child's hand (to ensure that the pressure remains the same) and then playing through all the possible bow placements – from the hazy flautando sound over the fingerboard right down to the hard edgy 'noise' that the bow can make next to the bridge.

By doing this the teacher will be able to demonstrate to the student the important fact that these areas do not all serve the same purpose in terms of sound. He might at the same time awaken in the pupil a fascination for the many colour and texture differences he can get through the way he uses this space with his bow. It is essential that this little game should be repeated frequently throughout the early years of playing so that the awareness of these possibilities will be kept alive and nurtured throughout the pupil's development.

Legato bowing

As I explained earlier, the application of the forefinger against the stick is the means by which the bow is held into the string and creates the sustained bow in legato playing. An awareness of this principle should be made a part of the cello pupil's thinking from the earliest stages, so that his use of it can develop as his playing develops.

Bow changes in legato playing can create problems because cellists, in striving to get the changes as smooth as possible, can be tempted into making contrived finger and wrist movements on the bow to camouflage the bow change. The impetus to do this may arise partly from the pupil having observed this kind of finger and wrist movement, or what appears to be this kind of movement, in more advanced cellists and then attempting to re-create it. Smooth bow changes, however, are not the result of contrived wrist and finger action on the bow, but rather of a hand that is so loose on the stick that as the arm turns around and takes another direction, the fingers continue on in the previous direction for a split second before going with the arm in the new direction. The principle is much the same as one sees in a paintbrush, where the bristles, because they are relaxed and have no will of their own, follow after the movement of the brush handle, wrist and arm. (Anyone who has watched the movement of seaweed underwater as it sways with the push and pull of the tide will have the perfect image in his mind.)

String crossings and legato playing

It is a common habit for cellists, even at advanced levels, to play with the bow squarely mid-way on each string and then make a quick flip when they change to an adjacent string. But, as the photographs opposite begin to suggest, there are infinite degrees of angle that the bow can have on any string. It is manoeuvrability within those degrees, and command of that space, that makes possible the smoothness of line in legato playing when string crossings are necessary.

The subtle directional sense, the veering towards the string one is going to play on next, even through the course

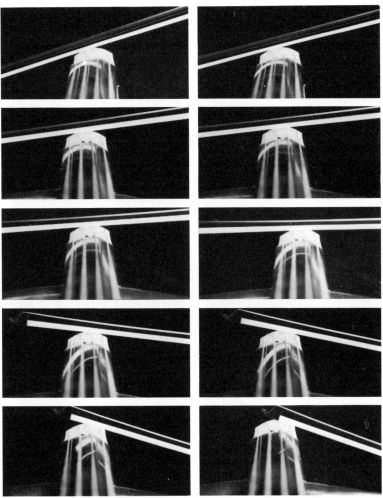

A few of the degrees of angle that the bow can have between the D and G strings

of many notes and bow changes, has parallels in many things we do in life; it is a physical economy which is almost instinctive in human beings and animals. But it is used too little in cello playing. The result of abrupt changes of angle is a jolt or splash in the sound when the bow moves on to the next string which completely destroys any sensation of legato (something which is particularly noticeable on the A string because of its sensitivity). It is from this kind of indiscriminate action that one gets so many bad string crossings, creating so many false accents that jut out of the musical line.

These diagrams show how this 'jolt' can come about in a crossover from the D to the A string if one starts from the 'far side' of the D and moves abruptly to the 'far side' of the A string. To avoid this, the cellist should, throughout the course of notes he is playing, angle gradually with the

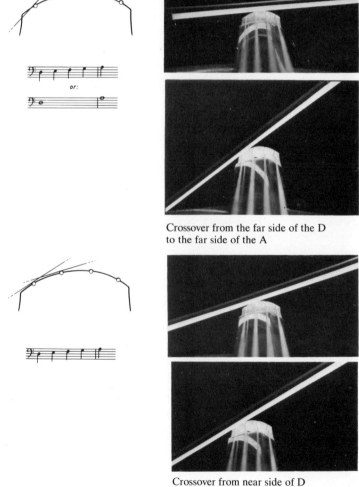

Crossover from the far side of the D to the far side of the A

Crossover from near side of D to near side of A

bow towards the A string so that the actual crossover, when it comes, is almost imperceptible (as shown in the second diagram).

The accompanying photographs show this in actual playing: the first two illustrate a move from the far side of the D to the far side of the A string. The second two illustrate the smoother crossover from the near side of the D to the near side of the A.

There are many excellent studies for the cellist to use in the investigation of string crossings, starting with the scale or even open strings. Studies like the Popper No. 2, and many other similar études, offer ideal concentrated examples for the cellist to work out, as is apparent in the opening two bars:

The instruction to the cellist in this study is, 'With very steady bow', but he will never be able to have a 'steady bow' unless he first investigates the subtleties of string crossings – smoothness of string crossing goes hand-in-glove with the creation of a steady bow. He should actually take the exercise even further and investigate the arm and hand movements in string crossing when in the lower half and the upper half of the bow, what gentle undulating movements he can get when alternating back and forth between two strings. This logical curving of the angle of the bow during the period of time on any one string is the foundation of perfect legato in string crossing.

Spiccato bowing

Before one ever gets down to teaching a pupil spiccato bowing in earnest, one should encourage the pupil first to enjoy the fun of experiencing the natural bouncing properties of the bow. It should delight children (of all ages) to play around with this natural tendency of the bow.

When the student is ripe for using spiccato in a serious way, he should be given a taste of the living experience by having the teacher place a hand over his hand and guide it to a natural feeling for the intrinsic bounce in the bow and the control of this bounce. (To do this, the student's hand must remain completely relaxed inside the teacher's hand.) Then, as the teacher slowly takes his hand away, the student will be more able to continue the movement on his own – it becomes easier for him because he has already felt it as a living sensation. As with the teaching of vibrato, this is a situation where words can only take on meaning after the pupil has already experienced the sensation of movement. From there, he can be guided to the infinite degrees of subtle control he will need to have over the bouncing bow.

Teaching vibrato

This same method of guidance may be used to advantage when teaching vibrato. The teacher, by slipping his hand over the pupil's hand, will be able to give him the living experience of the sensation before he has had a chance to intellectualize about it. If one just talks about vibrato, it does not get the pupil very far; but once he has 'tasted' it, once he has felt the sensation in his own hand, then the teacher can gradually begin to let go and the pupil will be able to carry on. There is little purpose in trying to explain in words a feel which has no counterpart in words. Nor is there any value in giving the pupil empty exercises before he can relate those exercises to something he has experienced. The living experience gives birth to an innate understanding, which the teacher can *then* build on in words and through exercises.

It is important, however, that students should not be allowed to learn vibrato before they have first learned to develop an expressive sound in their right hand and have fully understood that the source of all sound is in the bow. Otherwise the temptation to 'prettify' the sound with vibrato will be too great. In many students the urge to learn vibrato actually arises from a dissatisfaction with the sound they are producing and from the mistaken belief that all it needs to make it beautiful is a little vibrato. This is not only the wrong reason for vibrating, but it can easily lead to an inexpressive one-gear vibrato, while at the same time undermining the cultivation of an expressive bow technique. Often one does not need much vibrato to fill out the sound (even a slight vibrato can be very full within a thin thread of sound), but cellists must learn from the start to relate their vibrato to the sound they are producing and to the expressive content of the music.

Four
Practising in the Early Stages

The early stages in practising are ones of considerable development for the young pupil, and because of this the teacher has to become very involved in helping him to develop correct disciplines *vis-à-vis* the way he practises.

Although the circumstances of modern living make it difficult, if not impossible, for students to have two lessons a week (especially at the beginning), I do think that this is the most desirable way, for then the teacher can exercise more control over the pupil in the early stages and guide him towards right ways of practising when he is on his own later. A week is a very long time for a child (even an older child) to work on his own when he is learning a new craft. We do not ask this of him in any of his studies in school (imagine a child learning maths by having one lesson a week and then doing the rest on his own!) and yet the discipline and skill he will acquire in the process of learning a musical instrument will be of no less value to him in later life – whether he becomes a musician or not – than the skills he learns in his school subjects. He is not just learning to play the cello, he is learning a highly disciplined craft. In the process he is developing his expressive powers and capacity, and these are skills which will make anything else he does in life both easier and more meaningful.

Establishing discipline in practising

The establishment of a routine in the early stages of practising is a necessary discipline builder, but the teacher has to find disciplines for the beginner-pupil which are a *variation* of the adult disciplines he will have later on.

There are many things which are not 'hard discipline', which perhaps do not even look like discipline at all in the adult sense of the word – but which will help to build a sense of discipline in the child (the word discipline is itself such an adult word – almost harsh). There are gentle disciplines which adults have forgotten about because of their developed stamina in life, but the seed of discipline in the child needs to develop slowly from these gentler disciplines into the harder ones he will need for adult life.

Practising away from the cello

From the very beginning the pupil should be made aware that not all his practising is going to take place on the cello. Rhythmic understanding, for instance, can often be learned to better advantage away from the cello. Apart from the little rhythmic games one can play with youngsters, there are other ways of working away from the cello that will develop with the pupil and follow him into adult life. Pupils should be encouraged to sit down with the metronome and develop the ability to tap or beat or clap varying numbers of notes within the beat. Even more advanced players need to do this kind of exercise so that they develop the ability to execute complicated rhythms easily, and to slip smoothly from three to four beats within the bar (or any other combination) while still retaining the inevitable logic of the beat. The stronger these foundations, the easier these groupings become as one encounters them in increasingly difficult situations in cello playing.

The teacher has to recognize that balanced separated study (study away from the cello) needs to develop in relation to the pupil's growth and expanding capabilities. The horizon always recedes into the distance, and rhythms, pitches and other aspects of playing will all become more complicated as the pupil progresses. The craft of playing the cello does not become easier because one has learned the basics; those basics are just the *starting point* for something which is going to expand endlessly. As the pupil increases his technical command on the instrument, the teacher must see to it that the parallel growth of separated study is not allowed to wither and die.

Practising away from the cello can also include the earliest steps that will lead later on to proficiency in score study. Even young pupils are capable of understanding the structural lay-out of their simple pieces. They should be encouraged to look at the music away from the cello and to discover for themselves the musical 'lie of the land' – a kind of musical 'map-reading' in simple form.

Finally, pupils should also be encouraged to sing the tunes of their studies and pieces when they are away from the cello. By doing this they will not only develop a more natural and musical relation to what they are playing on the cello, but will also begin to prepare the soil for later improvising and for memorizing.

Improvising and memorizing

I have already suggested that as a child begins to understand and master scale-pattern fingerings, he should be encouraged to improvise new fingering patterns. This will stretch his imagination regarding fingering possibilities and at the same time expand his knowledge of the fingerboard. Development in this direction can lead logically into further improvisations of little tunes and snatches of scale and arpeggio motifs. He can be encouraged as well to play the melodies of songs he knows by memory, setting them in different keys to stretch his knowledge still further. Improvising and playing tunes by memory will not only help the pupil to develop a spontaneous way of handling the cello, but will lead him towards a more complete existence on the cello. In addition it will strengthen his ability to memorize because his association with making music on the cello will not be confined to eye-hand co-ordination and rote finger movements generated by the printed page.

Finally, and most importantly, by practising in this way

the young cellist will begin to let the ear take over as the guide to what he does on the cello. Instead of rushing always to the music and looking to the visual stimulus of the black dots on the paper, he will learn to fuse finger action with ear imagination, and finger memory with ear memory – so that the ear, not the eye, becomes the generating power behind his playing.

Five
Assessing and Guiding Talent

Everyone has the right to want to be a musician, but it is the obligation of the teacher to help each person sort out his potentialities *vis-à-vis* the many pathways in music he could take. In the world of professional music there are many paths, and most people (if they are suited at all) are not going to find each equally compatible with their abilities and inclinations. There are also many paths in the non-professional world of music, many ways in which music and ability on an instrument can serve simply as an added enrichment to life. Until a decision is finally taken, all the doors should be kept open. But, in the process, it is the obligation of the teacher to help the student in assessing his aims and inclinations in relation to his abilities.

Before one starts to teach someone, it is first important to meet with him and through talking with him find out how he thinks and what kind of a person he is. One needs to know what ambitions he has (or are they even his?), whether his desire to become a musician is a healthy one, or whether it is for the sake of glamour, or any number of other unhealthy reasons (with very young children it will be partially the parents one is assessing). Even if the reasons appear to be unhealthy ones, one must understand the various ways in which these can be handled and not lose sight of the fact that many fine talents who later turn out to be good musicians can start out with immature ideas. It is up to the teacher to probe in a way that enables him to discover not only whether that person's attitudes are healthy at that moment in time, but whether they can *become* healthy, and whether his potential justifies his (or his parents') ambitions.

It is usually difficult to make all the correct judgements and assessments on the spot. But if the first meeting convinces the teacher that there is potential, then he should advise the pupil or his parents to begin lessons on the understanding that there would be a reassessment again after a three- or six-month period.

Reassessing one's goals in the light of one's development on the instrument is a process which should go on for a considerable time. Reassessment is particularly important for talented pupils in their late teens who, because of the demands of school work, have not had a chance to work as intently on their instrument as they should and therefore have no proper basis upon which to make a good decision.

A realistic decision on this level is made even more complicated by the fact that a pupil who is talented in music often has talents in other areas, and will need a breathing space to step back and get the fullest picture he can in order to weigh his potentials and his inclinations properly. In these cases, his talent deserves that he take one year off for intensive work and then reassess himself at the end of that year. He can then rethink his situation in terms of his progress and can at the same time observe the growth or change in his attitudes towards his ambitions. (All this will be judged in the light of an extra year of maturing as well, which is important.) This year of assessment is a very critical one for both the student and for whoever is teaching him, but it is essential.

I feel it is wrong for teachers to encourage into the profession people who do not have the abilities, the drive, the self-discipline and the stamina to sustain them in whatever path they choose. One has to understand that the large teaching establishments on the college level do not have the powers of sifting and assessing students to the same degree and on the same kind of personal basis that can exist between teacher and pupil. This is why the greater responsibility rests upon the individual teacher not to send students into situations for which they are ultimately unfitted (perhaps for reasons having nothing to do with talent or ability) just because an institution, with its more superficial screening processes, has accepted them for study.

Six
Parents Beware!

By whatever means a child is brought into contact with a musical instrument – be it through the school orchestra needing another cello, through the stimulation of something he has seen or heard, or through the parents' love of music and music-making in the home – it is healthier at the beginning to allow the child a period of relaxed exploration through fields of sheer enjoyment in his first contact with an instrument and with music.

The first months should be for the child like wandering in refreshing and tantalizing pastures. Parents must therefore resist the temptation to make his lessons and practising an ambitious part of his study curriculum right from the start. They should instead use the first year as a time to learn about the child, his attitudes *vis-à-vis* the instrument, and his attraction to that particular instrument (as far as that can be assessed). If they can stand back a bit and adopt this kind of attitude, they will have a better chance of not killing off his interest from the start.

After all, the ordinary school routine is already a form of gentle pressure, however well it is done, and I think that to add music studies in that light is to make them appear in the young mind as further pressure. The child should never be made to feel in the early stages that his music studies are yet another item in his daily list of 'musts'. The art and craft of playing a musical instrument should be used instead as a life-giving antidote to the other type of study. From the beginning the child must be allowed to see that playing an instrument and making music are much more related to the things that are lovely in life, not the duties of life – and, where possible, that they are related to the activities of family life.

The first few months on an instrument (the exact length of time is very much dependent on the child and the situation) should be an exploring period for the parent and the child. If the child does not happen to have the greatest cello schooling in that period, there will be no harm done (providing neither the teacher nor the parent put on him the sort of pressures which would destroy the contentment of his innocent wandering through these new fields).

Later on, after allowing the child's contact with the instrument and with music to develop naturally and having assimilated the insights they have gleaned regarding the child's attitudes, the parents should give their first serious thought to the choice of a teacher. It could be to continue with the teacher who started him, but the parents should seek the best advice available to them and should not hesitate to go to the finest musicians they know of for an assessment (in so far as one is possible at that time) of the child's possibilities, and for advice on the right teacher to develop those possibilities.

Under no circumstances should the parents think, or allow themselves to be seduced by anyone else into thinking, that this study is going to be for 'professional' reasons. This is a dangerous mentality which causes parents unwittingly to sow ambitious seeds and unknowingly to put pressure on the child. Parents do need to be concerned, but their concern should be discreet, something the child is not even remotely aware of – far from creating a sense of pressure, it should be more like a gentle current the child can ride on. Parents must learn to stand outside – not in a neglectful way, but in a gentle, stimulating way. This is an attitude which is very much dependent upon the wisdom of the parents. If the child even begins to get a hint that he is being put under pressure, then the parents will be starting on the lowest rung of the ladder as far as healthy encouragement to the child goes.

Parent, child, teacher

There has to be a balance between the parts played by
the parent and the teacher in the child's learning and
development. Parents, however well-intentioned their
efforts, can exert pressure which will push the child away
from a healthy, intelligent development, by destroying the
parent–child–teacher partnership on which any healthy
foundation has to be built. Unfortunately, whenever the
partnership goes wrong, it is always the child who is the
victim.

Parents need to understand that the child's guide at the
start has to be the teacher and not the parent. Even in
practising at home, parental interference and influence can
be dangerous: first, because the parent may over-estimate
his or her own musical knowledge and understanding and
interfere with what the teacher is trying to teach the child;
and secondly, because his or her interference can be
psychologically dangerous for the child in the early years
of his association with an instrument.

By 'psychologically dangerous' I am referring to the fact
that most parents are facing this situation for the first time
in their lives and therefore cannot always evaluate the
deeper issues in this particular area of the child's development. In any situation parents are never in as full control
of the child as they think they are: and, particularly in the
area we are talking about, the only real control they can
exert is that of stepping back and observing the natural
development of the child without setting any rigid timetable for him which is possibly out of step with his nature,
inclinations, instincts and talents.

The danger exists not only for parents who are either
non-musical or amateur musicians: parents who are professional musicians face a whole new set of dangers
growing out of their musical and professional prejudices
(which none of us can escape), and an unconscious ambi-
tiousness on behalf of their child. They, more than any
others, must closely examine their own reasons for wanting

their child to carry on in the profession. On the whole I find them to be more often guilty of not allowing the child the latitude he needs in his development; they want the child to 'get right down to it' since they themselves have had their teeth into it for so long.

All parents, however, can and should meet frequently with the teacher and discuss with him the child's growth. Both parents and teacher can pass on to one another invaluable observations and insights.

The fallacy of the time factor

In school the child is under pressure to keep pace with his classmates in whatever subject they are learning. But it is a great mistake when this 'keep pace' mentality is carried over into a child's development on a musical instrument. There is no absolute time factor written in the Scriptures, the way some grading systems in music would suggest. One child may develop very quickly at the start, but lack the ability or inner capacity to blossom out later, while another may show a certain amount of talent which only comes to full bloom later on. There are many different forms of flowering, and many different time factors in flowering; there are many different ways of allowing a little human being to flower and bring his musical personality into existence. The variation is limitless.

This is why I am particularly critical of grading systems for young children in music. Not only do they tend to establish in people's minds a yardstick that is linked to a timetable, but they also cause people to look at grades in a narrow way, which often makes them an obstacle to the child's musical development.

Grades and balance

When the idea of taking an examination is first presented to a child, he may be enthusiastic and think it is an exciting thing. He may already be wanting to do it because his friends at school or in the Saturday orchestra are doing it and he wants to be like them. But it is important that the parents assess the temperament of the child and understand that many children are turned away from continuing on an instrument through insensitive timing relative to the development of the child at that time. A child should never be made to run before he has learned to walk. Nor should he be used as a pawn in his parents' ambitions. You can kill a child's love of music-making through fear and pressuring. Some children, of course, thrive on examinations, but others react in a way that can be detrimental to their progressing in a healthy way: for them the exam becomes only a psychological hurdle in their path.

Both the teacher and the parents must keep an eye on balance in a child's relation to the craft of playing an instrument, so that the desire (his or theirs) to excel in an examination does not outweigh the music-making aspect. Often it is very much a question of knowing how to handle the delicate balance between how much the child gains from the jumping of the examination hurdle and how much of his love of pure music-making gets destroyed in the process. Certainly there is no objection to letting a child have the fun – and sense of accomplishment – of jumping hurdles (*if* it is fun to him), but the hurdle-jumping should always take place within the balanced context of playing with and for friends, so that a child sees his music-making first and foremost as a source of getting and giving pleasure and fulfilment.

We are touching here on the question of what the *parents* (or teachers) want their children to achieve and why. It is all too easy for parents to deceive themselves about the measurements given out in the syllabus. Parents feel so close to a goal when they look at the sequence of Grades one to eight* – it seems such a short step on paper – that they become greedy for this kind of superficial achievement and develop a foreshortened view of the

*I am, of course, referring to the English system here; other countries may have their equivalent systems, but the principles remain the same.

whole spectrum of playing an instrument and making music. They are induced, by systems of external evaluation, to believe that grading a child's ability on an instrument is a simple and straightforward matter. They have been deceived into thinking that a grade is a measurement of where the child has got to – and it is *not*. The blind eye that is often turned on the child's reaction to examinations is frequently due to this kind of false evaluation on the part of the parent or teacher.

I see this kind of blindness often in young people who come to me for advice and ask me whether, now they have passed their grade 7 or 8 examination, I think they are ready for something like the Schubert Arpeggione Sonata. They have been led up the garden path by the illusions (or delusions) fostered by the grading system and have no idea of the many worlds of techniques they still have to go through to achieve the level of a work of this difficulty. The easy look of the grading system has undermined theirs and their parents' vision and has trapped them into a situation where they are looking at the world of musical performance through the wrong end of the opera glasses. Both the student and his parents have to realize that they must look at the grading system in a much wider, and *wiser*, fashion. It is not just a matter of 1–2–3–4–5–6–7–8–*star*!

Attitudes toward music competitions

The attitudes engendered by the grading system can become the germ for wrong thinking which extends to the competition as well. One has to accept that students in this day and age are to some extent forced into competitions by the simple fact that they exist – and by the fact that external success is a part of one's musical existence (though I still maintain that anyone with real individuality and musical ability cannot really be kept down, whether he ever enters a competition or not).

Given this situation, young people and their parents

need to recognize and understand that there are unhealthy aspects to competitions. It is clearly not art for art's sake any more; the unconscious eye is on some other goal – money, recognition, success. It helps to breed a sort of corruption and at the same time may discourage the development of certain good qualities which have not yet had time to fulfil themselves in a young person – and which he may then never discover. There are time factors in every person's development that should never be interfered with, and the timing of a competition may be contrary to those factors and detrimental to his natural development – you cannot conquer time.

There are many questions the young player has to ask himself when he thinks about entering a competition – questions his parents and teacher must encourage him to ask. Is he looking for a short-cut to fame? Is it the money? Or is it (more healthily) the incentive to make him work? How realistic is he about his ability in terms of the competition? (I mention this because I am often amazed at people who enter competitions completely ignorant of the standard of playing that will be expected of them.) Is his ability to cope with a successful win at that moment, and his ability to handle further career progress, out of step with the rest of his development? (Success often brings such pressures that if it is out of alignment with the development of the personality, the evolving of the whole musical person may be stunted or somewhat distorted.) Is his ambition to enter a particular competition out of step with the timing of his own personal and technical development, so that the intense pressure he puts on himself to attain the one goal actually works to the detriment of the more basic aspects of his musical (and personal) development? Will he be so pressured in reaching out for an objective that when he has achieved it, he will not be able to step back into the natural flow of the healthy continuity of development of his musical personality and art and allow himself to blossom in a more natural manner? (One has to accept that all preparation for competitions is like forcing growth in a hot-house.) I think there has to be a lot of soul-searching by the young person and his parents for the answers to these questions.

I would say that if one cannot take the knocks lightly, one should try to develop one's career in a different way. Young people need to bear in mind that there are many great performers about today who never went in for a competition. But if a young person *does* go in for a competition, what is really important is why and how he goes into it. I think that the recent emphasis on competitions misleads a lot of young people and their parents into becoming greedy about it without stopping to think about the damage it could cause to the individual. People should understand that the person who has the best competition temperament is not necessarily the best musical person. Conversely, there are people with temperaments which are most musical, and who are technically wonderfully equipped, but for whom competitions provide the wrong kind of stimulus; their temperaments work completely differently in a competition from when they are in an actual performance.

Winning competitions can be a bit like winning a lottery – and one knows what this kind of chance winning can do in destroying one's values and one's sense of balance in life. Of course in musical competitions the element of luck is more contained, but there still *is* an element of luck, and the person going into a competition must understand this. That is why I often say to young people entering competitions, 'Don't let the fact that you lose lead you to undervalue yourself, and don't let the fact that you win delude you into thinking that you are terrific'.

In the final analysis, the competition is a form of patronage by luck. And as a form of patronage it shows itself to be a weaker and less healthy type than the proper patronage of the private individual who can recognize a talent and give it a healthy opportunity to develop and perform in step with its own natural growth.

Part Four

The History and Repertoire of the Cello

One
An Introduction to the History of the Cello
Nona Pyron

(Readers who are interested only in the history of cello performance are advised to begin with Part Two of this chapter (page 224).)

Part I: Origin and early history of the cello

Although the violin, complete in every essential aspect, first appeared in artistic depictions in the late twelfth or early thirteenth centuries, the 'bass violin', or what we would now call the cello, did not come into being until the fifteenth century. The reason for the late appearance of the cello is related to the 'sound ideal' in Western Europe in the Middle Ages which, until the fifteenth century was high-pitched and nasal. Singers then used their voices in a way we would now associate more closely with Eastern music – and the instruments which accompanied those voices (for this was the principal function of instruments then) were designed to produce a similar sound. At that time the bass voice was simply not a part of our musical concept.

In the mid-fifteenth century, however, composers of the Flemish school began to extend the vocal range downward, eventually reaching low C where, for practical reasons, it has remained ever since.

At approximately the same time, perhaps even motivated by the same impulses, there was a shift in the sound ideal to the more open-throated sound we are familiar with today. It is no accident that at precisely this time in history the first *bass violins* begin to appear.

208

Are the bass violin and viola da gamba related?

It might be useful, before we go further into the history of the cello, to touch upon the relationship between the bass violin (or cello) and the bass viola da gamba. The history of these two instruments has often been so closely intertwined that it is important to clarify the basic differences between what are, in reality, two very distinct families of instruments: the viols and the violins.*

Although it has been a widely held belief in recent centuries that the cello *descended* from the viola da gamba, the two instruments appeared at approximately the same time and via two very different lines of descent. The cello is in every respect a violin – only the dimensions are larger – but the gamba is apparently a direct descendent of the 'Meccan lute'. This ancestry is suggested in part by the number and tuning of strings, and in part by the basic shape of the sound box.

Whereas the early violin had three or four strings, tuned in fifths, the viol (like the lute) had five or six strings, tuned in fourths with a third in the middle. And while the shape of the violin was established in the twelfth or thirteenth centuries in the form of a figure-eight, or two conjoined circles, the gamba, in its earliest form, appears to be directly derived from the lute (with bouts cut in the sides to accommodate the bow, and a flat back to facilitate holding – though some early depictions show viols with vaulted backs like the lute). The relationship between the viola da gamba and the lute was apparently perceived to be so close in the early sixteenth century that when Hans Gerle, in 1532, illustrated these bowed instruments, he called them 'lutes'.

Apart from the number and tuning of strings and the overt shape of the sound box, there are other important structural differences which affected the sound of the

*Throughout this preface the term 'violin' will be used in the generic sense, as it was prior to the mid-eighteenth century, to designate *all* members of the violin family, from bass to treble.

instruments and which further link the viols to the lute, and serve to distinguish them from the violins.

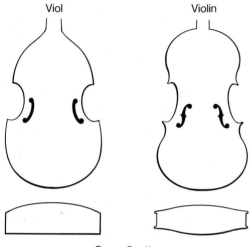

Cross Section

1. Arching: whereas the arching of both the front and back of the violins was very prominent, viols had flat backs and gently curved bellies.

2. Overlap: on violins there is an overlapping 'lip' which extends the arching of the front and back out slightly beyond the ribs, while the front and back of the viols tend to fit flush with the ribs.

3. Corners: the curve set in motion by the shoulders of the violins continues outward to produce distinct corners, whereas the shoulders of the viols slope directly downward to the point where the bouts cut inward, without any outward curve (or at most only the slightest suggestion of a curve). (The corners of the violins, incidentally, are a decorative addition of the Manneristic period which, because they are so pleasing to the eye, are copied to this day in spite of the fact that they serve no functional purpose, being filled with blocks of wood to keep the original 'figure-eight' shape of the sound box.)

4. Ribs: the ribs of the violins tend to be narrower than those of the viols (in all sizes of instruments from bass to treble).

5. Sound holes: generally speaking, violins had f-shaped sound holes and the viols c-shaped, though in the fifteenth century there was no complete uniformity on this. Many viols, and some cellos, also had a third sound hole in the shape of an intricately carved circle ('rosette') in the centre of the belly beneath the fingerboard.

6. Frets: violins were generally without frets (though there are some notable exceptions), whereas the viols were usually fretted. This was more than a surface point of distinction, as we shall see later on.

These differences between the two families of instruments are often clearly discernible in paintings, drawings and other artistic depictions of the period. Because of this, pictorial representations from the early centuries of the cello's existence, such as the two shown below, afford us some of our best information.

However diffused the lines of demarcation between the

An early cello

A viola da gamba

early viols and the early violins may have become in subsequent centuries, in the early sixteenth century the distinctions were clearly perceived and insisted upon with a persistent tenacity. And however obvious our backward glance may make the relationship between these two families of instruments seem – particularly between the bass members of those families – the viola da gamba, in construction, in tuning, and in terminology, is an instrument of distinctly different background from the cello.

Even the name 'violin' is rooted in the Latin 'fidicula', whereas the derivation of the name 'viola da gamba' indicates connections with the Arabic language and the Meccan lute (though via a circuitous and almost certainly unintended route). Around 1500 the Meccan lute in Spain was known by the Arabic name 'kabus'. When pronounced, this sounded like 'ganbus'. Since 'vihuela' was a common name for almost any bowed stringed instrument in Spain at that time, the bowed version of the lute would almost certainly have been called the 'vihuela de kabus'. Given, too, that the Arabic habit of playing bowed stringed instruments was to hold them in a vertical position on the legs, it takes little imagination to foresee that when the bowed lute reached the Italian courts (via Spain's close links with Naples and Milan), the Italians would have interpreted 'vihuela de kabus' (pronounced 'vihuela de ganbus') as 'vihuela de gamba' or, to complete the Italianization, 'viola da gamba'. This appellation would have seemed quite fitting as the instrument was held on the legs while playing, and the Italian word for leg is 'gamba'.

Early terminology underlies important differences

The tradition in string playing in Western Europe throughout the Middle Ages and early Renaissance had been to hold the instrument on the arm or shoulder and the bow with an overhand (palm-down) grip. The viola da gamba, imported from Spain where Arabic influences prevailed, brought with it, as we have just seen, the tradition of holding the instrument in a vertical position and the bow with an underhand (palm-up) grip. Throughout the six-teenth century and well into the seventeenth century terminology intended to distinguish between these two groups of instruments chose to root itself in this difference in holding position. Thus, the violins came to be called 'viole da braccio' (arm viols) and the viols 'viole da gamba' (leg viols). To these names were frequently added the further descriptive terms of 'con trastes' (i.e., with frets) and 'sin trastes' (i.e., without frets) to indicate that the viols were played with frets while the violins were not. The stressing of these two points – holding position and presence or absence of frets – was of vital importance to the sixteenth century mind, for it implied a great deal about both the derivation and the nature of the sound of these two distinct families of instruments.

Within the two families, the instruments were further delineated according to their voice ranges: descant (or treble), alto, tenor and bass. Thus, a 'cello' in the sixteenth century would have been called 'basso di viola da braccio' (with possibly 'sin trastes' added on for good measure) or simply 'basso da braccio'. Nearly all sixteenth-century writers group these instruments in this manner, though some make it clear that there is often more than one size of instrument within a given voice range.

The seventeenth century was well under way before this terminology began to give way. In 1607 Monteverdi, in his opera *Orfeo*, still orchestrates for ten 'viole da braccio' in ensemble music scored in five parts from bass to treble. And in 1636 Marin Mersenne* explains that the famed *24 Violins of the King* consists of six trebles, six bass, four altos, four tenors, and four 'quints'.†

*Mersenne, *Harmonie Universelle*, Paris 1636. Substantial parts of this have been translated into English by Roger E. Chapman: Marin Mersenne, *Harmonie Universelle*, 'The Books on Instruments', The Hague 1957.

†'Quint' is a puzzling term about which there is no universal agreement amongst music historians today. It seems probable that this name refers to the five-stringed bass violin which was tuned like the cello, but with an added bass string tuned a fifth below the lowest string. Praetorius,

The significance of frets

The musical significance of frets manifests itself in two ways: the effect they have on the quality of the sound produced; and the relationship they have to intonation and to the capacity of an instrument to modulate to foreign keys.

To begin with the first point: when one plays a fretted instrument such as the viol, the string is stopped by placing the finger slightly *behind* the fret so that the string is pulled taut over the fret; thus it is not the finger, but the fret itself, which actually stops the string and produces the tone. The sound which results from this method of stopping is cool, clear, refined and somewhat impersonal. The *violins*, on the other hand, lacking frets and having their sound produced by direct contact of the finger with the string at the point of stopping, produce a sound which is generally assessed to be warmer, more personal, more amenable to nuance and having more of the qualities of the human voice. Thus, purely in terms of sound, the distinction between the fretted and non-fretted instruments is a very real one, and one which was to have increasing implications as time went on and musical tastes evolved (ultimately, as we know, to the disadvantage of the viols).

The relationship of frets to intonation is equally important for quite different reasons. A fretted instrument is, unavoidably, a *fixed-pitch* instrument in the sense that the player can do little to alter the pitches once they have been determined by the placement of the frets.

Early keyboard players, who had to wrestle with the problems of a *fixed-pitch* instrument, expended vast amounts of time and thought on ways of 'tempering' the tuning of their instruments so that they could avoid the

---

in 1619, seems to confirm this by listing amongst the viole de braccio an instrument tuned which he called 'Gross Quint-Bass'.

harsh clashes of intonation brought about by the so-called 'Pythagorean Comma'.* Without tempering, an instrument which was well tuned in one key could be outrageously out of tune in a distant key, but by 'cheating' slightly the keyboard player could distribute the discrepancy of the Pythagorean Comma over a range of many octaves. Thus tempering was a way of 'splitting the difference', a compromise which would help smooth out harsh tonal disjunctions without too great a cost to the overall sense of intonation. (Bach's *Well-Tempered Clavier* was an attempt to illustrate that a 'well-tempered' instrument could play in all twenty-four keys without any great intonation problems.)

But while keyboard players found their solution to the problems of a fixed-pitch instrument in tempering, no such solution was available to the gamba player, as frets could hardly be adjusted sufficiently to accommodate complicated tempering systems. Thus, as composers began modulating to foreign keys, gambists found themselves confronted with increasingly insurmountable problems of intonation, while violinists, free from the confinement of frets, were able to adjust their pitches to the tonal demands of virtually any succession of chords.

Mersenne is quite specific about this in his *Harmonie Universelle* (1636) when he says:

The violin. is one of the simplest instruments that can be imagined, in that it has only four strings and is without frets on its neck. That is why all the just consonances can be performed upon it, as with the voice, in as much as one stops it where one wishes. This makes it more perfect than the fretted instruments, in which one is forced to use some temperament and to decrease

---

*'Pythagorean Comma' is a term given to the pitch discrepancy which occurs when one has come full circle – or *should* have come full circle – in a cycle of fifths. To wit, when twelve successive perfect fifths have been played, one should, in theory, be returned to the starting pitch (albeit some octaves higher), B-sharp being the equivalent of C; but in actual practice one finds that a B-sharp thus obtained is a discernibly higher pitch than the original C – this difference in pitch is known as the Pythagorean Comma.

or increase the greatest part of the consonances, and to alter all the musical intervals, as I shall later show. . . .

It must still be noted that the violin is capable of all the genres and all the species of music, and that one can play the enharmonic, and each species of the diatonic and chromatic upon it, because it carries no frets, and contains all the intervals imaginable, which are in force on its neck, which is comparable to the primal matter capable of all sorts of forms and figures, not having any fret at all on the violin that produces a particular tone. Thus is must be concluded that it contains an infinity of different tones, as the string or line contains an infinity of points. . . .*

Later he says of the viol:

The parts of the viol are similar to those of the violin. . . . it differs . . . only in that it has frets which limit its capacity and which, from the infinity which it might have, determines it in seven or eight equal semi-tones which are made on its neck by means of the eight frets. . . .†

A century and a half later, in *The Practice of Fingering the Violoncello*, John Gunn writes:

The violin was not only better adapted to produce a proper effect at each of these places, from its greater strength and brilliancy of tone; but was found, on trial, when put in the hands of artists of skill, to have a power of producing a more perfect harmony than had ever been done by the viols. This arose from a cause that had not probably been before suspected, namely, that the fingers, by practice, and the guidance of a good ear, effected a more accurate intonation, than could ever have been accomplished by the direction of frets, fixed on the fingerboard with the utmost mathematical precision. These can never be so applied, that the intervals or stop can be exactly in tune, but in one key; in every other, they will be remarkably faulty; and if the error be divided and lessened by what is called temperament, the variation from exact tune will be easily distinguishable and offensive to a correct ear.

*Marin Mersenne, op. cit., Proposition I, pages 238–9 in the translation by Roger E. Chapman, The Hague 1957.
†Ibid., p. 249

The three sizes of the early cello and how they were tuned and held

As we have seen, the earliest 'cellos' (more correctly, 'bass violins') began to appear in the mid-fifteenth century. Pictorial evidence makes it clear that by the beginning of the sixteenth century various bass violins (alongside many experimental forms) were commonplace in musical settings. From these and other sources we also learn that the 'bass violin' came in roughly three sizes (more or less corresponding to the bass, baritone and tenor voices) and that these were held variously across the breast or resting upon the calves of the legs or upon the ground. This photograph shows three extant instruments in the three sizes.

The three sizes of the early cello

The Cello

Michael Praetorius, in 1619, gives the tunings of the three bass violins as follows:*

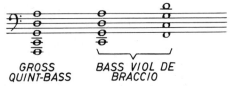

GROSS
QUINT-BASS

BASS VIOL DE
BRACCIO

Other sources, and the music itself, sometimes indicate tunings of the two lower instruments a whole tone lower than Praetorius's. Thus the middle bass could also have been tuned

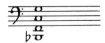

Since the pitch of the 'Gross Quint-Bass' is identical with that of the modern cello except for the added fifth string, it is clear that Praetorius does not have a *contra* bass instrument in mind. The tuning in fifths would also rule out the possibility of this instrument's being transposed down an octave.

For those readers whose eyebrows went up at the mention of an early 'cello' being played while held 'across the breast', let me re-emphasize the importance which appears to have been placed at that time upon the idea of the 'da braccio' position. Since the bass violin was, after all, an 'arm viol', it must have seemed only natural that it should be played 'on the arm' (or at least as close to that position as one could get, given the size of the instrument). Actually, the smallest bass, which was quite a bit smaller than our modern cello, did not present insurmountable difficulties in this respect; and the largest bass was usually held in a vertical position (considerations of precise terminology giving way to anatomical necessity, though one is surprised to see on more than one occasion depictions of these very large instruments held horizontally). What *does* confound our modern mind is that the middle-sized bass violin, the instrument most analagous in size to

*Michael Praetorius, *Syntagma Musicum*, Wolffenbüttel 1619.

218

our modern cello, is also frequently held in the sideways position.

A beautiful illustration of this position occurs in a fresco in the loggia of the tiny chapel of Roccapietra near Varallo in Northern Italy. There, on facing walls, are depictions of two bass violins, the larger held in a vertical position and the smaller across the breast.

Cello held in horizontal position

Large 'cello' held
in vertical position

Other depictions from the sixteenth century indicate that this sideways position was not at all uncommon at this time. Indeed, cellos were often suspended sideways across the breast of the player by means of a ribbon or hand, as in the picture below. The cello, when played in this position, was quite possibly called the 'viola da spalla', a term which has puzzled historians, but whose definition – 'a large stringed instrument held across the breast and suspended by a ribbon or band' – fits perfectly.

Cello suspended across
the breast

The Cello

Seventeenth-century terminology

Early in the seventeenth century a new terminology for the violins began to develop, existing side-by-side with the old terminology for several decades (to the general confusion of all). Discarding the old 'da braccio' forms, the new nomenclature chose the word 'viola' as the central pillar of its system: from there it branched out in both directions to provide names for the smaller and larger 'violas'. This was accomplished by the use of the Italian diminutive (*-ino*) and augmentative (*-ono* or *-one*) endings, hence: violino=small viola; and violone = large viola.

Had there been only three sizes of instruments in the violin family at that time, as there are today (violin, viola and violoncello), then this terminology would have proved quite adequate and complete. But there were, as we know, at least *five* sizes of violins in common use in the early seventeenth century. While Praetorius, in 1619, lists tunings for three bass violins of graduated size, the word violone can account for only *one* instrument larger than the viola.

The problem of naming them was solved in the following fashion: the smallest bass, which served the voice role of tenor in ensemble playing, was given the name 'tenor' for the remainder of the seventeenth century (by the eighteenth century, however, the term 'tenor' usually indicated the viola proper); and the middle-sized bass was simply called a 'little violone' (i.e., 'little large viola'). The Italians accomplished this semantic legerdemain by the simple device of adding a diminutive ending to a word already possessing an augmentative ending. Thus, if 'violone' was the augmentative of 'viola', then to get a 'little violone' the simple thing was to add on a diminutive ending to 'violone', link it with a connecting consonant, and presto: vio*loncino*. Some Italian dialects used *-elo* or *-ello* as a diminutive ending, and *z* sometimes replaced *c* as the linking consonant, so that in the 1640s we find the small violone – our cello – variously indicated as *violoncino, violonzino, violonzelo, violoncelo* and *violoncello*. It was, of course, this latter version which eventually stuck and which became the name by which we know this instrument today. The shortened version 'cello' was used as early as 1765.* Italian terminology notwithstanding, the name 'bass violin' for both the violone and the violoncello remained popular in the north of Europe, where these instruments were known variously as 'Bass Geige' (Germany), 'Basse de Violon' (France) and 'Bass Violin' (England), until well into the eighteenth century†

The name 'violone' eventually became so confused with the largest member of the viola da gamba family, especially in northern Europe, that composers often had to make a point of specifying which instrument they intended. In 1696, one composer, who signed himself only as 'J.A.C.', used the preface to a series of instrumental pieces to point out that by 'violone' he meant the 'four-stringed bass violin', thus confirming the existing confusion at that time. This confusion of terminology regarding the violone is still with us today.

The demise of the violone, in the early part of the eighteenth century, coincides with the rise of the contra bass in instrumental music. Stradivarius made his last violone (specified in the books usually as a 'large model violoncello') in 1710. And Corelli replaces the violone with a violoncello in the second edition of his Op. 3 Sonatas.

The violone, violoncello and tenor

Since all three 'bass violins', the violone, the violoncello and the tenor, were quite probably played by 'cellists' in the seventeenth century, the relationship between these instruments is of particular interest for cellists today. Although information is still scant and incomplete, it is becoming increasingly apparent that the tenor – which grew in size from about 65 cm. body length in the early

*C. P. E. Bach, *Fugue pour Violon, Alto et Cello* [sic], Brussels, Bibliothek National, BC V 15, 242.
†1737 marks the year when Walsh Publishers in London replaced 'Bass Violon' with 'Violoncello' in their publications.

seventeenth century to about 70 cm. in the eighteenth century – was probably used by cellists as a solo instrument.* The four-stringed version was usually tuned G d a e′ and the five stringed version C G d a e′. Since by the mid-eighteenth century the violone has ceased to figure heavily in musical performance, or in instrument making, it is even conceivable that when Quantz refers to the need for cellists to possess two instruments – a larger one for continuo playing and a smaller one for solos – he actually had in mind the violoncello and the former tenor (which by then had grown to become a small solo cello).

By the beginning of the nineteenth century the cello was becoming increasingly standardized to the size we know today, and the terminology gradually confined to the single name 'violoncello' or the shortened version, 'cello'. Most of the larger violoni have since been cut down to produce instruments conforming with this standard, and many of the small cellos (formerly tenors) have been enlarged – or left as they were and sold as 'half-size' cellos for children (a concept, incidentally, which was apparently foreign to people's thinking in earlier centuries).

The cello as 'bass'

Only one further etymological hurdle remains to be jumped, and that is the persistent reference, particularly in the eighteenth century, to the cello as 'bass', or 'basso'. It is an important point because many modern performers and historians have fallen into the trap of believing that this term meant 'contra bass' or 'double bass'. The fact is that when composers in the eighteenth century meant contrabasso, they said contrabasso – and when they said 'bass', they were nearly always referring to a cello.

It is not uncommon to see a work with 'violoncello' printed on the title page and then find the actual part labelled 'basso' – or vice versa. Other sources confirm this

*Lowell Creitz at the University of Wisconsin, Madison, has done extensive research on the 'tenor', and his findings should soon shed important light on this instrument.

usage. The official instruction book of the Paris Conservatory, also reprinted in Leipzig in German, states: 'The bass is to be considered in a double sense. As a solo instrument it is called violoncello, and as an accompanying instrument it is commonly called bass.'*

Some composers used the term 'bassetto' or 'Bassetchen' when referring to the accompanying violoncello. Boccherini's father often toured with him, accompanying him on the 'bassetto', which was probably one of Quantz's 'continuo cellos'.

The practice of equating violoncello with 'bass' grew out of the seventeenth-century habit of allowing wide latitude in the instruments used for playing the basso continuo line. Often the music itself specified that this line could be played by bass violin, a bassoon, a bass viola da gamba or a chitarrone. When this was not explicitly stated, it was nevertheless still implicitly understood, unless the composer actually specified a particular instrument.

In the late seventeenth and early eighteenth centuries, as the concept of idiomatic writing took increasingly greater hold, it became more and more usual for composers to indicate a specific instrument for a given line. (Corelli, as we have seen, specified that a violoncello was obligatory for the bass line in the later editions of his Op. 3 sonatas.) Thus, many of the 'violoncello obbligato' parts in the early eighteenth century, which surprise us because they lack the virtuosity we have come to associate with the word *obbligato*, were in reality only attempts on the part of the composer to exercise control over the choice of instrument for the bass line (and hence over the tonal colour of the ensemble). They were only making it clear that in that particular instance a violoncello (or whatever instrument was named) was 'obligatory' on that part. (Later in the century the word *obbligato* took on a different meaning and seeing 'with violoncello obbligato' on the title page

*Baillot, Levasseur, Catel and Baudiot, *Méthode de Violoncelle et de Basso d' Accompagnement*, Paris 1804.

generally meant that the cello had a virtuosic solo part – either throughout the piece or at some point within it.)

Part II: The history of cello performance

As we have seen, the earliest cellos begin to appear in paintings in 1440–50, and it is mainly through pictures, augmented by written documents and references, that we gain our understanding of this earliest period of the cello's existence. Incomplete as it is, this information is considerable enough to allow us to form some idea of the first 200 years of cello performance. While many details are still hazy, the larger contours are nonetheless discernible.

From written and iconographical evidence we now know that the cello (known then as the *basso di viola da braccio* or *bass violin*) existed in three sizes, with appropriate tunings, and that it was held either horizontally across the breast or vertically upon the calves of the legs or upon the ground.

Praetorius, as we have seen, gives the following tunings for all the violins ('viole de braccio', which he also calls 'Geigen').

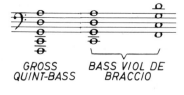

GROSS QUINT-BASS   BASS VIOL DE BRACCIO

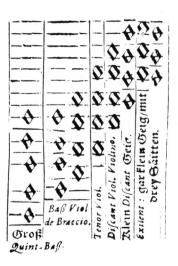

It was not unusual, incidentally, for any of these instruments to have five strings in the seventeenth and early eighteenth centuries.

When and where the early cello was played

The association of the 'violins'* with matters sacred goes back to the Middle Ages, and from the Renaissance onward they were used regularly in church services and in religious ceremonies and processionals. In the fifteenth, sixteenth and seventeenth centuries artists' depictions of celestial choirs were rarely without violins (of all sizes) in the hands of angels. However, when Tinctoris states (in 1487) that he would prefer to see the violins reserved 'solely for sacred music and for secret consolations of the soul, rather than have them sometime used for profane occasions and public festivities', he thereby implies that their use was not confined to religious music. Actually, the 'violins' spanned both worlds with equal ease and from the sixteenth century onwards could hardly be dispensed with in either religious or profane spheres. 'Profane occasions and public festivities' ranged from weddings and other ceremonial processions and banquets to raucous music-making in the village taverns, and from aristocratic dances in the noble courts and stately homes to rustic festivities in the towns and hamlets (such as those depicted on pp. 226 and 228).

Of particular interest to cellists is a contemporary elaboration on just how the larger 'violins' were carried in ceremonial and festive processions:

Il est aussi plus facile a porter, qui est chose fort necessaire, mesme en conduisant quelques noces ou mommerie.

L'Italien l'appele violon da brascia ou violone, par ce qu'il se soutient sus les bras: les uns avec escharpe cordons, ou autre chose, le bas a cause de sa pesanteur est fort malayse a porter,

---

*Using 'violins' in the generic sense, as it was used in the sixteenth and seventeenth centuries, to denote all members of the violin family from bass to treble.

Playing for 'profane occasions and public festivities'

pour autant est soustenu avec un petit crochet dans un aneau de
fer, ou d'autre chose, lequel est attache au doz dudict instrument
bien proprement; a celle fin qu'il n'empesche celui qui en joue.

The violins are also easier to carry, and this is very important especially when conducting a wedding or a mummery.

The Italians call it violin da brascia or violone because it is held on the arm; by some with a scarf, tape, or something like that; the bass, on account of its weight, is very difficult to carry and is therefore supported by a little hook in an iron ring or something similar, which is attached very neatly to the back of the said instrument, in such a way as not to impede the player.

Jambe de Fer, Epitome Musical, 1556

The engraving at the top of p. 228 shows bass violins being carried in this manner in processions. The one below it is of especial interest because it is from a plate showing the 'Orchestra of Tritons' from Beaujoyeulx's *Balet Comique de la Royne* (1582), which was the first music specifically to mention *violins*. The music for the *violins* was scored in five voices, from bass to treble.

Whether in the service of the church or aristocratic houses, or whether in the more earthy environs of the public taverns and village squares, contemporary accounts seem to indicate that the violins were played mainly by 'professionals':

Nous appelons violes celles desquelles le gentilz hommes marchantz et autres gens de Vetuz passent leur temps. . . . L'autre sorte s'appelle vilon et c'est celuy du quel l'on use en dancerie communemant et a bonne cause. . . . qu'il se trouve peu de personnes qui en use, si non ceux qui en vivent par leur labeur.

We call viols those [instruments] which gentlemen, merchants, and other people of quality play as a pastime. . . . The other kind is called violin and is commonly used for dancing. . . . except for those who earn their living by it, few people play it.

Jambe de Fer, Epitome Musical, 1556

Although the violins were apparently not held in the highest esteem by Jambe de Fer (and presumably others), they nevertheless spread throughout Europe with astonishing speed, and by the end of the sixteenth century had established themselves in a position of musical prominence.

Playing for 'profane occasions and public festivities'

The cello in the seventeenth century

While the violoncello continued to be used in many of the ways already established in the sixteenth century (especially in the church and for dancing), from the early 1600s onwards it appears to have become very popular for music-making in the home by people of all classes. Painters depicted people of all ranks of society playing the cello, and in many settings one sees the cello very much at home in the hands of amateurs who are clearly playing for pleasure, as for example in the paintings reproduced on pp. 229 and 230.

On these occasions cellists played in small ensembles with one or more other violins or wind instruments. But they also played alone and even accompanied themselves while singing. Roger North, in his *Memoirs* of *c*. 1700, gives the following description of the use of the cello in seventeenth-century London:

'There was a society of gentlemen of good esteem . . . that used to meet often for consorts after Baptists' manner and performing exceedingly well with bass violins (a cours [sic] instrument as it was then, which they used to hire), their friends and acquaintances were admitted, and by degrees, as the fame of the meeting spread, so many auditors came that their room was crowded, and to prevent that inconvenience, they took room in Fleet Street, and the Taverner pretended to make formal seats, and to take money, and then the society disbanded.'

In the church and in the chamber the cello was not only an indispensable member of ensembles of violins, but

'Concert à la compagne', unknown artist

performed equally well and often in ensembles of mixed wind and string instruments. Many cellists, such as G. B. Vitali in the mid-seventeenth century, were held in high regard for their ability as composers as well. In fact, from this time onward until the end of the eighteenth century, it is rare to find a performer who did not also compose.

'Music-making in the home', Adriaan van Ostade

The cello and the growth of the violin repertoire in the seventeenth century

One of the mysteries of music history is that when idiomatic virtuoso writing for the violin began to develop in the early decades of the seventeenth century, and the sonata and related forms mushroomed into existence, there was no rise of an equivalent repertoire for the cello. Historians from the late eighteenth century onward have taken this to mean that cello playing was in a more primitive state of development at this time than was violin or viola da gamba playing: they presumed the cello to be a clumsy and cumbersome instrument which could be played only in the most rudimentary fashion and reasoned that it could have coped with nothing more taxing than the basso continuo line (the six Bach Suites notwithstanding) until late in the eighteenth century, when Boccherini, discovering its solo potential, transformed the caterpillar of the violin family into a butterfly.

Edmund van der Straeten* repeatedly states (and is quoted endlessly by subsequent writers) that the level of technical achievement on the cello was only of the most primitive sort and could not in any way be compared to that of the violin or viola da gamba. Yet he himself often cites evidence which points to a quite different conclusion. (To name just one example: the virtuoso 'duel' between the cellist Tonelli and the violinist D'Ambreville in the early eighteenth century was so spectacular that the audience 'broke out in rapturous applause at the end'.) Certainly it is difficult to believe that cellists, surrounded as they were by capable colleagues on the treble violin and gamba, could have remained uninfluenced by the burgeoning virtuosity exhibited all around them. Indeed, they would have had to be blind and deaf, and completely lacking in any sense of musical adventure, not to have developed a commensurate virtuosity on their own instrument. The evidence points to the conclusion that they did.

*E. van der Straeten, *History of the Violoncello, the Viola da Gamba, their Precursors and Collateral Instruments*, London 1915.

The Cello

Assessments which see early cello playing as 'primitive' and 'technically backward' probably reflect more the apparent lack of repertoire for the cello in the seventeenth century and, perhaps, an incomplete understanding of the extent of the cello's own repertoire in the early eighteenth century.

The discrepancy between the great volume of music for the violin in the seventeenth century and the dearth of it for the cello can be best understood in the light of two factors. First, idomatic writing for a specific instrument was only just beginning to develop in people's thinking; and secondly, even the early idiomatic writing for the violin did not necessarily exclude the deeper voices of the violin family. Cellists, considering themselves to be 'violinists' (albeit 'bass violinists'), quite naturally adopted the violin repertoire as their own (transposing it down an octave), making no more distinction between the various voices within the family of violins than do singers today with their solo repertoire.

Given this, it is easier to understand why a cello repertoire equivalent to that of the violin never emerged from the seventeenth century – nor is ever likely to emerge. This also helps us understand why cellists of the eighteenth century were so conversant with treble clef, and why the practice of writing cello 'solos' in chamber music in treble clef carried on well into the nineteenth century. Here is an example of this early use of clefs:

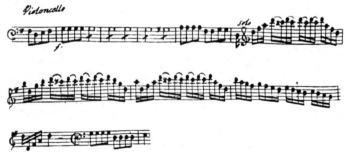

G. B. Cirri: String Quartet, Op 17, No. 6, *Allegro Spiritoso*

It is easy to understand as well why cello virtuosi were often considered on a par with violin virtuosi in the early eighteenth century, and why there remained in the eighteenth century such a large body of sonata music in the treble clef for either violin or violoncello.

The earliest music written specifically for the cello

When the first cello repertoire did begin to appear, it is likely that it was at least partially in response to a need for a middle ground to fill the gap between the relatively simple music of the bass lines and the increasingly demanding violin repertoire. Certainly, as such it would have given cellists who were not virtuosos a repertoire which was technically within reach, while providing those who aspired to the virtuosic heights a good solid ground upon which to develop their technical muscles and daring.

The first piece of music specifically written for cello (to be more exact, *violone*) was composed around 1650 by Giovanni Battista Vitali, himself *Suonatore del Violone*, and is entitled *Partite sopra diverse Sonate*. Vitali never published these partitas, and whether they were intended for performance or merely as exercises is difficult to ascertain. But by the 1680s Domenico Gabrielli and other cellists were beginning to publish sonatas and ricercari specially for the cello, and these were followed a decade later with compositions by Leonardo Leo, Cattaneo, Jacchini and Taglietti.

By the early 1700s the dam had burst and music specifically for the cello – sonatas, concertos and other compositions which treated the cello in solo fashion – flooded forth in an ever-increasing tide. As the cello separated itself from the violin repertoire, the former 'middle ground' rapidly expanded to take over the musical territory previously occupied by the virtuoso violin repertoire as well. Before the Baroque era had come to a close, thousands of works had been written for the cello. Rarely since has the cello enjoyed such a rich and varied repertoire.

From a manuscript copy by Hannelore Müller: an extract from Domenico Gabrielli's *Ricercar No. 6 for Violoncello Solo*

The relationship between the cello and the viola da gamba in the seventeenth and early eighteenth centuries

The viola da gamba quickly gave way to the cello in Italy and by the mid-seventeenth century travellers to Italy remarked that it was scarcely known there any more. But it remained the preferred instrument in the north of Europe, particularly in France, until well into the eighteenth century, many gambists resenting the cello as a rude and rambunctious rival.

Yet however great the preference for the gamba in some northern lands, the superior tone of the cello (superior in terms of the evolving sound ideal) had not passed unnoticed by the gambists. As early as 1659 Christopher Simpson in his book *The Division Violist* illustrates, as reproduced below, two possible body shapes for the viol and tells his readers that the first (almost identical to the cello) is to be preferred because it is superior in sound. Ultimately the tide of changing musical taste was too strong and went too deep to be stemmed by superficial modifications of the gamba; by the beginning of the eighteenth century gambists everywhere were beginning to abandon their instruments in favour of the cello or (like the famed gambist C. F. Abel) becoming proficient on both instruments.

From Christopher Simpson: *The Division Violist*

Because many gambists who changed to the cello found the reasons for changing their bow grip not compelling enough to alter a lifelong habit, one sees with increasing frequency at this time depictions of cellists playing with the palm-up bow-hand position (the palm-down position had been traditional with all violinists from the very start). It was not until cellists from Italy had fully infiltrated the music-making in Northern Europe that there was a return to some degree to uniformity in the bow-holding position.

Virtuoso cellists from Italy, travelling and performing in the north, overwhelmed their colleagues and the musical public with their unsurpassed skills. Hubert le Blanc, one of the gamba's greatest defenders, exclaimed, '[these] violoncellists, who have vanquished by hard work such immense difficulties that it makes one shudder to hear them prelude. One must admit they are most estimable, but not that their instrument is agreeable.'

Le Blanc wrote an impassioned plea on behalf of the viola da gamba (*Défense de la Basse de Viole Contre les Entreprises du Violon et les Prétentions du Violoncel*), but it was in vain. The cello eventually replaced the gamba in both ensemble and solo playing and the gamba dropped out of use until its revival in the twentieth century. The reason for the demise of the gamba in the eighteenth century lay less in its intrinsic merits or demerits than in the relentless unfolding of musical tastes and ideas. The succeeding musical eras, as we now well know, had little use for the cool, delicate qualities of the gamba and turned increasingly to the more robust nature of the cello, with its almost unlimited potential for emotional expression.

Cello playing in the late seventeenth and early eighteenth centuries

By the end of the seventeenth century the cello served virtually every important function it does today, plus many inherited from preceding centuries which have since passed out of practice. From the development of the concerto grosso onward no orchestra was complete without its cellos (usually both sizes in the early orchestras, *violoni* and *violoncelli*), and chamber music of every size and description depended upon the cello more than on any other instrument for the bass line (though in many ensembles the cello played the middle and upper lines as well). Cellists played in opera orchestras and in court orchestras, in private and in public concerts; they played for dances and for ceremonial functions; they played in church services and in religious processions, in homes and gardens of great refinement and in the bawdiest taverns and on village greens.

'Gentlemen' no longer confined their attentions to the viola da gamba, but made the cello the centrepiece of their musical entertainments and their family portraits. It became the fashion for people of high position to become patrons of aspiring cellists and to sponsor the publication of their music. Even the Prince of Wales was an enthusiastic amateur cellist, and numerous sets of sonatas were dedicated to him by composers for the cello; an example of this is shown on p. 238.

Virtuosi such as Lanzetti travelled the length and breadth of Europe, moving audiences with the beauty of their music and thrilling them with their technical mastery. The cellist Franciscello was so revered as a virtuoso that the violinist Franz Benda journeyed to Vienna to study with him and, so we are told, adopted his style completely. By the early decades of the eighteenth century both the cello and the violin had attained dominant positions as solo instruments, and technical mastery grew to proportions that have scarcely been surpassed in succeeding centuries.

Cello music in the late seventeenth and early eighteenth centuries

While treatises, first-hand accounts and pictorial depictions are even more plentiful and informative in the eighteenth century than in preceding centuries, it is the abundance of music itself which gives us, for the first time, real insight into the range and scope of the actual playing. Music manuscripts and early publications, more than anything else, put us in direct contact, musically and technically, with cello performance of that time.

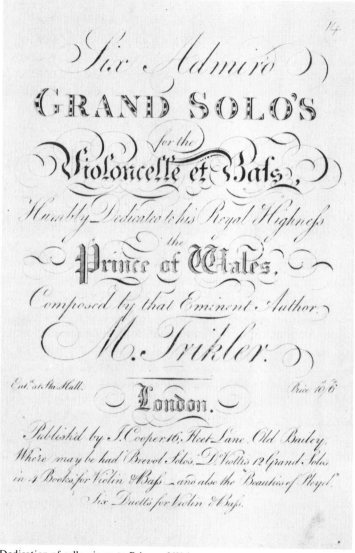

Dedication of cello pieces to Prince of Wales

Apart from the orchestral repertoire, the music played by seventeenth and eighteenth century cellists fell into seven main categories:

1. *Sonatas and 'Solos'.* In the late seventeenth century and throughout the eighteenth century the term 'solo' usually meant a composition for a melodic instrument accompanied by basso continuo or sometimes only a bass instrument. (The term 'basso continuo' encompasses both the instruments which played the bass line, usually harpsichord and a bass instrument such as the cello, bassoon or viola da gamba, and the realization of the harmonies implied by the figured bass.)

This music not only exploited the virtues of the instrument, but also gave cellists a solo repertoire which was roughly commensurate in difficulty with the then current violin repertoire. We have to remind ourselves that throughout the lifetime of Corelli and Vivaldi the violin repertoire, with some notable exceptions, tended to avoid the higher positions; yet cellists, playing on a normal four-stringed cello, would have needed very high positions to play this same music. The excerpt on pages 240–41 from Valentini's Sonata Op. 8, No. 1, which was published for violin *or* violoncello in Rome in 1714 and in London in 1720, shows how this music looked to the cellist.

The earliest repertoire specifically for cello, however, avoided this high level of technical command while sacrificing nothing of the beauty and profound sentiment of the violin repertoire. Being technically more accessible and yet musically of the highest quality, this new repertoire was equally suited for concert performance or private enjoyment by competent amateurs. (It is important to bear in mind that the demarcation lines between public and private performance, and between the professional player and the amateur, were more blurred than they are today – though even today there remains a wide 'grey area' between the two. In the upper classes of society proficiency on a musical instrument was a required social grace, and many 'amateurs' were technically and musically on a par with the

XII
SOLOS
for the
VIOLIN
or
VIOLONCELLO
With a
THOROUGH BASS
for the
HARPSICORD
Compos'd by
Giuseppe Valentini
Opera Octava

London Printed for I: Walsh Serṽ: in Ordinary to his Majesty at ỹ
Harp & Hoboy in Catherine Street in ỹ Strand. & I: Hare at ỹ Viol &
Flute in Cornhill near ỹ Royal Exchange ——

(Cellists played this transposed down an octave)

finest soloists. Often, in fact, it was the social rank of the musician, rather than his ability, which determined whether he considered himself a 'professional' or a 'dilettante'.) Thus much, if not all, of this early cello music might have been heard in a public concert hall, or in public or private concerts at court, or at a gathering in a stately home (with perhaps the host and some of the guests taking part), or simply for the private pleasure of the performers on their own.

By the third and fourth decades of the eighteenth century, however, there was a rapid rise in virtuoso solo music: sonatas and concertos which sought to exploit the technical and musical capacity of highly developed soloists in a repertoire written specifically for the cello. Sonatas by Barriere in 1733, for instance, show imaginative use of double stops and string-crossings; while compositions by Martino (probably Sammartini) of about the same time give clear indications of a highly developed thumb technique (a technique already familiar via the performance of violin sonatas on the cello).

Martino, Sonata in D minor. Second mov., bars 46–69

Sonatas by Paxton and others in the 1760s show a growing preoccupation with various possibilities of the bounced bow, as the old outward-curved bow began to be replaced by the straighter 'transitional' bows and eventually with the Tourte, or modern, bow. (Please see pages 264–5 for the distinction between the Baroque, transitional and modern bows.) In general, there seemed to be few

Jean Barriere: from the Sonata in D (1733)

limitations to the inventiveness and technical capacity of
eighteenth-century cellists. While style and sound concepts
have changed in recent centuries, very little has been added
to the basic technique since the eighteenth.

Stephen Paxton: Sonata in D, Op. 1 No. 6 (*c*. 1760), bars 1–15

2. *Cello Duos, Trios and Quartets.* In the Baroque and Classical eras duos for two cellos were a common form of music. If the frequency with which cellists appeared in concert programmes, and the glowing accounts of those concerts, are any measure, they were also an exceedingly popular form. In many duos, the second cellist took an accompanying role, as is illustrated in this sonata by Boccherini.

L. Boccherini: Sonata in A, for two cellos, *Allegro*, bars 1–6

But at other times the two cellists shared in equally virtuosic roles, as in these works by Lindley and Stiasny:

etc.

Robert Lindley: *Three Duets for Two Violoncellos*, Op. 1, Duet No. 1 in E-flat, *Allegro moderato* – bars 49–63

Jean Stiasny: *Trois Duos Concertans pour deux Violoncellos*, Op. 6, Duo No. 1, *Andantino*, bars 41–6

Other eighteenth-century composers, such as Cervetto, Kennis, Romano and Corette, wrote for groups of three and four cellos.

G. B. Cervetto: *Six Sonatas or Trios for three Violoncellos or Two Violins and a Bass*, Sonata No. 1, *Adagio*, bars 1–3

3. *Music for beginners*. By the mid-eighteenth century a wealth of music specifically intended for beginners, or

amateurs of limited ability, was being written and published. This was actually a branch of the solo and duo music we have been discussing, and usually took the form of easy duets for two cellos (often pupil and teacher). These simple pieces were satisfying enough musically to content players of higher musical aspirations while the development of their technique was *en route*. Because both the upper line and the bass were usually technically accessible to elementary players, they encouraged beginners to develop from the start the flexibility they would later need in playing both bass lines and upper melodies.

Most of the cello tutors of the eighteenth century utilized the duo as a major vehicle for teaching, and most were exceedingly imaginative in discovering ways to satisfy the musical appetite even at the earliest stages of playing. Oliver Aubert, as shown on pages 248–50, for instance, ingeniously sets a lovely melody for the teacher (or any other moderately competent cellist) to play against the very first whole-note scales of the beginner, and thus infuses into what might otherwise be dull scale practice a breath of the magic of musical creation by allowing even the beginner to taste the joy of making music. He then develops the scale into increasingly complicated patterns, each forming a kind of obbligato to the original tune.

Other tutors combine theoretical lessons with duo practice: *Il Maestro ed Il Scolaro*, by Stiasny, is a series of duos which also serve as studies in imitation at every interval.

4. *Concertos*. As the idea of the concerto as a vehicle for solo playing began to develop, composers wrote increasingly for the cello in this form. By the end of the eighteenth century many hundred concertos had been written for the cello (often by cellists themselves, but also by other composers who were apparently attracted by the versatility of range in the cello). Technically many of these concertos were extremely demanding and through them, as well as through the sonata repertoire, we gain a great deal of insight into the levels of technical competence required 200 years ago.

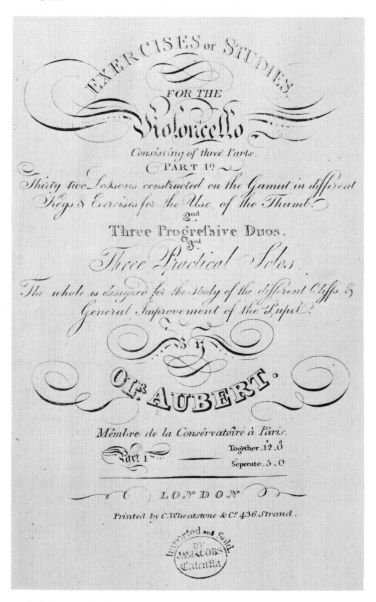

EXERCISES or STUDIES

FOR THE

Violoncello

Consisting of three Parts.

PART 1st.

Thirty two Lessons constructed on the Gamut in different Keys & Exercises for the Use of the Thumb.

2nd.

Three Progressive Duos.

3rd

Three Practical Solos.

The whole is designed for the Study of the different Cliffs & General Improvement of the Pupil.

Or. AUBERT.

Membre de la Conservatoire à Paris.

Part 1 ———— Together .12 .0
———— Seperate .5 . O

LONDON.

Printed by C. Wheatstone & Cº 436 Strand.

From O. Aubert, Exercises or Studies for the Violoncello

It is worth noting in passing that solo cellists at that time did not separate themselves from the orchestra as much as they do today. Often they were themselves leading members of the orchestra and in concertos played the tutti sections with the orchestra until it was time to enter with the solo part, returning again to the tutti when the solo part ended. Most eighteenth-century concertos, as shown by the example below, are scored in this fashion and by implication we can surmise that it was probably not usual for the cellist to memorize his part.

Haydn: Concerto in D, Op. 101, bars 1–48

Cadenzas then, as now, were an accepted (and expected) part of concerto performance, but were less separate compositions in themselves than elaborations on a series of chords leading to a final return by the orchestra. Tartini, in his *Traité des Agréments*, gives several skeleton forms for possible cadenzas, together with the kind of figurations that could be used to fill them in. (Please see page 76 for an example.)

5. *Chamber music.* In the eighteenth century chamber music carried a much wider range of implications for the cellist than it usually does today. As we have seen, cello duos were common fodder for cellists both for private enjoyment and in public concert (as well as cello trios, cello quartets and even some cello quintets). Duos with the violin or flute were also popular, as were trios for two cellos and violin, two cellos and viola, cello and two violins, and cello, violin and viola, and various combinations for cello or wind instruments. In addition to the instrumental music, masses and other sacred works of the late seventeenth and early eighteenth centuries frequently contain vocal arias with one or two violoncellos obbligato.

In the early part of the eighteenth century the string quartet was still in its formative stages – it did not crystallize into the form we know today until the end of the century. *En route*, however, there were many imaginative instrumental combinations, some of which must have been extremely satisfying for cellists. A fairly common instrumentation was for violin, viola and two cellos (the first cellist being paired with the violin in the upper voices and the second cellist providing the bass line). Cirri used this form of the string quartet to write a series of mini-concertos for the cello. Even in the standard quartet instrumentation, the cellist was given a much larger share of the solo role than was common in later quartets. (Please see page 232 for an illustration of this.)

6. *The Unaccompanied Cello.* As early as the 1680s composers had recognized the solo potential of the cello. The compositions of Domenico Gabrielli, Giovanni

Battista degli Antonii, Domenico Galli and Giuseppe Colombi are already beautiful examples of music for solo cello. But certainly the most sublime writing for solo cello, as every cellist knows, occurs in the Six Solo Suites by J. S. Bach.

7. *The Cello-Piano Sonata*. Finally, though it was a late eighteenth-century form which reached its full flowering in the nineteenth century, some mention must be made of the cello–piano sonata. This form, which made its first appearances in the last decades of the century, was not a continuation of the eighteenth-century sonatas for cello and basso continuo or two cellos alone, but grew out of a less important eighteenth-century form called the 'accompanied keyboard sonata'. (This same form was also the parent of the piano trio and, eventually, the piano quartet and quintet.) These sonatas were essentially pieces for keyboard – harpsichord and, increasingly as the century wore on, pianoforte – which had *ad libitum* parts for violin and/or cello by means of which solo keyboard playing could be expanded into a sort of chamber music when the other players were at hand. The Beethoven Sonatas, Op. 5, still show remnants of this approach. By the first decade of the nineteenth century the cello was placed on a more even footing with the piano and one finds true duo writing in the sonatas by Helene Liebmann and Joseph Woeffl (*c.* 1806) and in the A major Sonata by Beethoven (1809).

The accompanying cello in the seventeenth and eighteenth centuries

However fascinating it is to dwell on the prevalence of solo cello playing in the Baroque and Classical eras, we should not let our preoccupation with this aspect of cello performance blind us to the great use that was made of the cello as an accompanying instrument. The role of accompanist was a vital and highly esteemed part of every cellist's life in the earlier eras of cello playing.

Cellists participated then in vocal music to a degree which is unknown to us today: they were expected to accompany singers not only by playing the bass line, but by embellishing this with tasteful chordings and improvisations, and to be able to carry on and fill in when 'singers remain on the stage silent, because they have forgotten their part or for some other reason'. The cellist at such times 'may play short preludes and embellishments', but he is admonished to 'be modest therein, and use his ornamentations at the proper time and with taste'.*

To accompany well, the cellist needed to have a good understanding of harmony. John Gunn, writing in 1795, tells cellists that once they have mastered the rudiments of playing, 'it will be proper to proceed to the study and practice of accompaniment'. He then lists the three essential means to this end: one, the study and practice of tone; two, the study and practice of time; and three, 'an early acquaintance with pure harmony, and the habit of accompanying, and attending to, a part different from that of the bass'.

The method book of the Paris Conservatory in 1804 also stresses the need for cellists to have this knowledge and ability: 'To accompany a recitative well one must have a perfect knowledge of harmony as well as of the violoncello. One must be well versed with figured basses and be able to execute them readily. He who can do that has reached the summit of his art. . . .' The authors also warn cellists that 'if the accompanying bass player (violoncellist) is not sure in resolving dissonances, if he does not indicate to the singer whether he has to make a full cadence or an interrupted cadence, if he does not know how to avoid consecutive fifths and octaves, he runs the risk of embarrassing the singer and, in any case, will produce a bad effect'.

Quantz devotes much space to accompanying on the violoncello in his famous book,† warning cellists to be

---

*Baillot, Levasseur, Catel and Baudiot, *Méthode de Violoncelle et de Basso d'Accompagnement*, Paris 1804.
†J. J. Quantz, *Versuch einer Anweisung die Flöte traversiere zu spielen*, Berlin 1752.

particularly careful not to overpower the upper voice or voices with their improvisations and thus turn the accompaniment into a kind of solo. John Gunn also warns of the same trap awaiting the over-zealous cellist:

He will then observe how much it is in the power of the violoncello, by inattention to the other parts, to destroy their finest effects, and to counteract the most beautiful expression; and on the other hand, by a judicious management of [his accompaniment], how much fullness, mellowness and spirit, it can give to the whole, without injuring the softest passages, or most delicate expression, in any of the other parts. Hence it follows, that to accompany well comprehends the best use of the instrument, and constitutes the greatest praise of a performer; as it not only requires a command over the chief power of the instrument, but the utmost attention to be given to the other parts, as well as to his own, to enter fully into the spirit of the music and precise meaning of the performer, so as to give additional effect to it, but never to counteract, never to destroy or obscure it.*

Clearly, cellists in the eighteenth century were as much prized for their ability to accompany another voice or instrument as to execute difficult solos. Although Wasielewsky claims to have heard cellists accompanying in this manner as late as 1873, the ability to accompany on the cello was a dying art in the nineteenth century. In 1809 an article in the *Allgemeine Musikzeitung* states that 'the art of accompaniment [on the violoncello] has greatly decreased as players no longer study sufficient harmony'. The musical directions of the nineteenth century took cellists along quite different paths.

Taste and style in eighteenth-century cello playing

In the eighteenth century a great deal of attention and importance was given to good taste and a sense of style in playing. Geminiani's *The Art of Playing in a True Taste*

*John Gunn, *The Theory and Practice of Fingering the Violoncello*, London 1795.

(in which cellists, incidentally, are encouraged to practise the treble lines as well) is but one of many guides to mid-eighteenth-century string players on the details of performance to which they should direct their attention and which they should endeavour to develop in their playing.*

A sense of line was considered important at all levels of playing. Even beginner-cellists throughout the eighteenth century were encouraged to practise basso continuo lines, and to play them with the other voices, in order to develop a good understanding of line.

Style in eighteenth-century performance was not the cut and dried issue we often imagine it to be. Historical backward-glancing has a way of simplifying matters which were, in fact, anything but simple; the Baroque era did not come to a close and the Classical era begin as neatly on the stroke of midnight, 31 December 1749, as some history books would suggest. In actual fact the Baroque, Rococo and Classical styles lived cheek by jowl throughout the middle decades of the eighteenth century – and nowhere is this stylistic cauldron, with its ever-changing swirlings and bubblings of style and musical innovation, more evident than in the cello music of this time. Sonatas were commonly published in sets of six, ten, or twelve works and it is not unusual to encounter stylistically diverse compositions within the compass of a single set (although all were usually composed within a short span of time).

---

*The very fact that such emphasis was placed on style and taste is in itself a reminder to modern cellists that this should be their starting point, and their magnetic centre, as it were, when approaching music of this era. It is all too easy for players today, after reading a handful of treatises and slavishly trying to produce effects described therein without a real understanding of the broader musical issues, to develop grotesquely mannered performance habits in the sincere belief that they are playing an 'authentic' style. This approach blinds them to the central point of all eighteenth-century playing: that an understanding of the line, and a proper rendering of the line was all important. Graces and bowing nuances and articulations existed only to adorn that line and, by giving stress to certain notes, to make the contour of the line even more clear to the ear of the listener.

Familiarity with all the strands of musical thinking of the time was natural to every musician's understanding, and the music composed and played in these stylistically turbulent years provides very rich pasturage even today.

National styles, particularly French and Italian, were also an important consideration in eighteenth-century performance – and often, even then, proved a stumbling block to musicians versed in only one school. (One can only sympathize with Corelli when he told Handel, 'But my dear Saxon, this music is in the French style, which I do not understand.') The great discrepancy between the French and Italian styles in the eighteenth century led to heated arguments and pitched 'battles' in the concert halls of Paris before the issue was finally settled in favour of the Italian style. But even as the Italian style swept over Europe, the various cross-currents of historical styles continued their inter-weaving. It is only from the vantage point of history that we can see the broad mainstream of development out of the Baroque and into the Classical and eventually Romantic styles.

The transition to the nineteenth century

Sound concepts and instrumental techniques are always in the process of evolving and tend to move apace throughout the various periods of history. Thus it was, for example, that the changes in the bow which gave it greater springing ability and sustaining power grew out of Rococo ideas of melody and ornamentation. At the same time, the possibilities these innovations opened up must have had their influence, in turn, on the direction of later composition. All of these developments – in the instrument itself and in playing techniques – found their fulfilment in the Romantic love of rich sonorities, long soaring lines and often overt emotionalism. The cello, equally amenable to this world, became prized for its rich, warm tone and for its potential for emotional expressiveness.

Changes in attitudes towards performance were also taking place. For the first time groups such as string quartets were formed with the intention of developing a permanent ensemble wherein the members would perform together over long periods of time, developing in their performance a unity of heart and spirit as the contributions of the individual members were amalgamated into the expression of a single whole. Where the eighteenth century had prized spontaneity, improvisation and a sense of style and taste, musicians in the nineteenth century developed the ability to delve deeply into fewer works and thus bring to light hidden meaning that might escape a more superficial approach.

Part III: The modification of the cello throughout history

So far we have talked about the history of the cello mainly as it relates to performance. But the instrument itself, and the modifications which it underwent in the first 400 years of its existence, also had their effect on the history of cello performance. It is therefore perhaps well to break off this historical sketch at this point, leaving the reader to form his own opinions about cello playing in the present and recent past (as he will be inclined to do anyway), and direct our attention to the instrument itself and the way in which it has accommodated itself to changing musical styles and taste.

The interesting thing about the violin and the cello is that throughout the past 450 years the essential features and proportions of the main body of the instrument have not been altered in any substantial way. The only changes to the body itself have come from a tendency in the late nineteenth and early twentieth centuries to standardize the size of the cello, cutting down the larger violoni and enlarging the small solo cellos to make them conform to the norm of the middle-sized instrument (a tendency which, however well intentioned, has deprived us of the variety we might have in some of the finest instruments). But, even with these alterations, the basic shape and proportions of the sound box have been maintained.

The fittings (principally the neck, bridge and finger-board) *have* changed, however, and it is often through minute modifications of the fittings that the sound of the cello has been able to adapt to the changing ideas about sound throughout the centuries. From early sources we can establish quite clearly the way in which the neck was set, the height of the bridge and its curvature, the shape and length of the fingerboard. More speculative are the questions relating to the width of the sound-post and the size of the bass bar, about which there can be no conclusive answers (though from the original bass bars in existing instruments it appears that there was such a wide range in size in earlier centuries that it would be impossible to establish a norm).

Since most of the modifications in the cello relate to the amount of tension placed on the instrument, it is those fittings which control tension on the instrument which have been consistently altered. If we look closely at sixteenth-, seventeenth- and eighteenth-century paintings of cellos, we will notice that the neck is attached to the body of the instrument at approximately a right angle. As this position of the neck allows little or no room for clearance of the strings over the belly of the instrument, a thin wedge was frequently glued between the neck and the fingerboard to provide extra height. But even with this wedge, the height of the bridge on early cellos was still approximately 1 cm lower than on the modern cello. This lower bridge, together with the use of gut strings, a generally lower tuning and often a shorter neck gave the body of the cello considerably less tension than it has today, resulting in a sound that was relatively warmer, gentler, and less penetrating than that which we now associate with the cello.

The Cello

The 'sound ideal' in the Baroque era

While in our present age we tend to prize the cello for its 'rich, warm' tone and strive for an even bigger and more penetrating sound, in the Baroque era resonance was the quality most sought after in performance. Hubert Le Blanc wrote in 1740 that with good musicians, 'conjunctions of sound stir the air in the most perfect of proportions, so that with a few notes they achieve a most marvellous effect, causing the bronze ornaments on the vases to tremble, and setting up vibrations in resonant bodies'.

The sound produced by the Baroque cello was very much a child of its time, and the manner in which Baroque cellists played their instruments was governed both by the current sound ideal (which they shared) and by the resonances suggested to them by the instrument itself. A cello set up in the Baroque manner tends to resonate very freely when bowed with a light, easy stroke; this resonance has the particular quality of blending with the resonance of other instruments. Cellists sought this very beautiful resonance and developed bowing techniques which would help them achieve it. Thus sound ideal, the instrument, the music and the cellist's technique were part of a never-ending circle.

By the end of the eighteenth century, however, the piano was beginning its ascent to what would eventually be a position of instrumental predominance in the nineteenth and twentieth centuries. With the rise of the piano, a new kind of musical partnership sprang up – a new partnership which exercised a great influence on the modification of the cello – the cello–piano duo.

It is difficult for cellists today, who struggle to balance their instrument with the modern piano in the Beethoven sonatas, to realize that, with the keyboard instrument Beethoven had in mind, it was the *cellist*, not the pianist, who had to be careful not to overpower his partner. This state of affairs, however, did not last for long. The history of the piano throughout the nineteenth and twentieth centuries is one of ever-increasing dynamic and ever-expanding sound; and while the eighteenth-century cellos, with their gentler, clearer sounds, were match enough for the earliest pianos, as the piano sound grew increasingly louder cellists were hard put to keep pace. In seeking ways to modify the cello so that the partnership with the piano could continue, and knowing that greater tension on the body of the instrument created a harder-edged more penetrating sound and that a higher bridge meant more string poundage (and hence tension) on the body of the instrument, they increased the thickness of the wedge underneath the fingerboard to gain greater bridge height. Eventually, the thickness of the wedge reached proportions which made agility in the left hand difficult, so another solution had to be sought. It was found that by canting the neck backwards at a more oblique angle from the instrument, greater bridge height could be achieved with no restriction of the left hand. The line drawings below show the differences between a typical eighteenth-century cello and a modern cello.

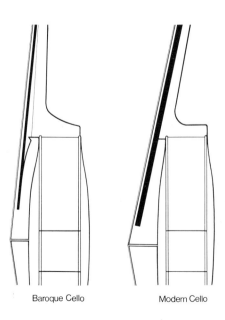

Baroque Cello   Modern Cello

The bridge, strings and pitch in early cellos

The actual shape and curvature of the bridge was different in the seventeenth and eighteenth centuries from what we are familiar with today. The Baroque bridge could be quite flat (to facilitate the chordings of continuo players), but it was also frequently as arched as the bridge we use today in order to give greater clearance for the intricacies of solo passage work (see the first of these photographs).

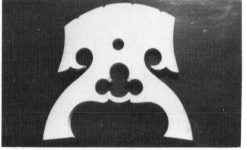

Baroque and Classical bridges

If one looks closely at early paintings one can see that some bridges in the Baroque era were quite heavy. By the end of the eighteenth century, however, the shape of bridges began to reflect the need for greater clarity of sound required by the Classical sound ideal. A typical bridge of the late eighteenth century is illustrated in the second photograph; comparison of it with the typical Baroque bridge shows it to be lighter, airier and less bulky than the Baroque bridge. The differences in sound are not enormous, but they do modify the sound enough to make it more compatible with the music of the period.

Strings and the pitch at which a stringed instrument is tuned also affect the quality of sound. Although steel strings have been in use since the sixteenth century, in the Baroque era they were used only in dance bands and for outdoor entertainment. For general playing cellists used uncovered gut for the upper two strings and silver or copper-wound gut for the lower strings. The thickness of the strings depended upon the size and set-up of the instrument and the purpose for which it was intended (continuo or solo playing).

Tuning varied a great deal in the seventeenth and eighteenth centuries. There were not only different pitches for church and chamber performance, but each country or region also developed its own idea of pitch. (This did not affect string players so much, but it made it quite impossible for wind players with instruments from different regions to play together.) In general the pitch was lower than we know it today, concert A being somewhere in the region of 415 Hz (instead of the modern 440 Hz).

The question of the end-pin

Although cellists in the twentieth century tend to regard the end-pin as an integral part of their instrument, it was not until the beginning of this century that it came into widespread use – which is to say that for some 350 years prior to this century cellists normally supported the instrument on their legs. There were exceptions, of course, and early paintings occasionally show a cellist with a short (usually ornately carved) stick supporting the instrument; but these examples are rare. More common, perhaps, was the use of a small footstool to rest the instrument upon. Or the cello, particularly the larger violone, could be rested on the floor while played. On occasion one sees depictions of cellists playing in a standing position with the cello resting on a chair or stool, but by far the most widespread holding position for the cello was that of cradling it on the calves of the legs.

The Cello

This is not such an uncomfortable position as some might imagine, and it has certain advantages which our modern position does not give us. For instance, because the cello, when held this way, is more vertical, the left hand gains a greater freedom and lightness of action which is particularly valuable in the fast passage-work of eighteenth-century music.

The evolution of the bow

Now what of the bow? Before François Tourte perfected the modern bow in the 1770s, the bow used in stringed-instrument playing had an outward curve. As such, it was a tool perfectly suited to the work it had to do. The Tourte bow, and the transitional bows leading up to it, are not necessarily 'improvements' over the earlier bow, but more the reflection of changing techniques generated by changing style and taste.

The Baroque bow (which is a popular way of saying the outward-curved bow) is ideal for achieving the articulations needed for Baroque music. Indeed, to achieve the same strokes, articulation and sound with a modern bow can be extremely difficult and often nearly impossible. The curve of the Baroque bow echoes the curve of the bridge, giving it a natural tendency to hug the string. This tendency is further enhanced by lesser tension on the hair (compared with the modern bow) and a more unequal distribution of the tension. The modern bow, with the curve of its stick opposing that of the bridge, and its greater hair tension, has a natural tendency to spring away from the string. This gives it two qualities which were required for music from the Classical era onward (qualities which were not inherent in the Baroque bow): the ability to play spiccato and the ability (through containing this natural energy of the bow by pressure with the forefinger) to sustain long expanses of melody.

Of course one can bounce a Baroque bow, but because this relies more on a lift from the hand and arm than the natural springing properties of the stick, the quality of the articulation is different. Similarly, it is possible to sustain melody with a Baroque bow, but here it is not so much a question of pressure with the forefinger against the stick (which would only choke the sound) but of setting up a resonance in the instrument with a relatively light stroke – literally *drawing* the sound out of the instrument.

The progression illustrated below shows the changes in the bow from the outward-curved Baroque bow through the transitional bow of the mid-eighteenth century (also ideal for the music of that period) to the modern bow.

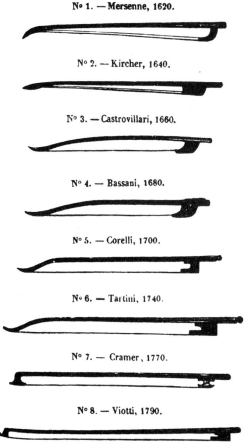

No 1. — Mersenne, 1620.

No 2. — Kircher, 1640.

No 3. — Castrovillari, 1660.

No 4. — Bassani, 1680.

No 5. — Corelli, 1700.

No 6. — Tartini, 1740.

No 7. — Cramer, 1770.

No 8. — Viotti, 1790.

Sequence of bows representing the development of the bow from 1620 to 1790

Finally, it is important for modern cellists to bear in mind that, while matters of instrument modification over the centuries can be discussed in a general way, and certainly the mainstream of development is clear, it is extremely dangerous to become too categorical about these changes. Knowing the degree of variation that exists in modern-day cellos in terms of the way they are set up, we should not be surprised that there was a similarly wide variance in instruments in previous centuries. Cellists did not march in lock-step to their local violin-maker to have their instruments altered periodically. The process of evolution is never tidy. But it does seem to be inexorable and eventually to catch up nearly everyone in its wake.

With the recent interest in music history and historical performance (the former a child of the last century, come of age in this; the latter a phenomenon of only the past decade or so), the attention of performers has turned not only to questions of appropriate style, but to performance on instruments which have been reconverted to replicate, as closely as can be deduced, the sound of instruments of a particular musical era. This, as already implied, opens up whole new areas for the modern cellist in terms of sound, style and technique. The vast amount of recently discovered music which was originally played by these early cellos opens up new vistas in programming and in our concept of ensembles.

As the opening up of these 'frontiers into the past' is combined with the imaginative opening up of new frontiers of sound by modern composers who are sensitive to the many still untapped potentials of the cello (I am not referring to knocking, banging and other gross abuses of the instrument but to the as yet unexploited range of sound within the legitimate use of the instrument), the present-day cellist finds himself in a position of almost limitless possibilities.

In the eighteenth century, cello performance (like all other musical performance) moved with the quickly changing times the way pop music does today; last year's compositions, with a few notable exceptions, went out of fashion and were relegated to the library shelves to make way for the 'latest tunes'. The same is true for much of the nineteenth century, though at a slower pace. From the late nineteenth century until the mid-twentieth century, however, cellists began to expand their sights backwards to include the music of the past. But at the same time they narrowed their sense of performance to force all this music into a single mould of sound and expression (even re-arranging the music of the past to suit this purpose). Now, for the first time, they are free to live properly in all worlds, to travel freely in their musical 'time-machine' and recreate through their instrument (or instruments, if they prefer) the beauty of the sound of any era of music from the Renaissance forward.

Recommended further reading

I. The history of performance

David Boyden, *The History of Violin Playing*, London, Oxford University Press, 1965.

While this book deals specifically with the history, performance and repertoire of the violin, so much of this information is equally pertinent to the cello that anyone wishing to extend his knowledge of the early history of the cello would be wise to begin here.

Edmund van der Straeten, *The History of the Violoncello, the Viola da Gamba, Their Precursors and Collateral Instruments*, London, William Reeves, 1915.

Though the historical view presented in van der Straeten's epic book is inaccurate in the light of subsequent research, the book still remains an invaluable source of biographical information on cellists in the eighteenth and nineteenth centuries. It also provides readers with many interesting and enlightening quotations from contemporary sources.

The Cello

Klaus Marx, *Das Violoncel und seine Spiel-Technik*, University of Münster Doctoral Dissertation (published), 1960.

This book (available only in German) presents a detailed history of the development of cello technique to 1800, based on contemporary sources. It also gives interesting information on etymology and other areas of early cello history. Written before the recent surge of 'authentic performance', the author's views on how the cello was held and played in earlier centuries falls victim to speculation not grounded in actual practice. But this does not detract from the wealth of other information for the serious reader.

II. The construction of the cello, and the history of violin-making

The following list comprises but a handful of the scores of books available on this subject:

Edward Heron-Allen, *Violin Making*, London 1889.
K. Jalovec, *Italienische Geigenbauer*, Prague 1957; original edition (Prague 1952) in Czech and English.
W. L. v. Lütgendorf, *Die Geigen- und Lautenmacher*, 2 vols, 4th edn, Frankfurt am Main 1922.
Otto Möckel, *Die Kunst des Geigenbaus*, Leipzig 1930.
Max Möller, *The Violin Makers of the Low Countries*, Amsterdam 1955.

Two
The Repertoire of the Cello
William Pleeth

Throughout the centuries the cello has been an instrument with seemingly endless possibilities both as a solo and as an ensemble instrument. Its wide compass, spanning over 4½ octaves through all ranges from bass to treble, and its enormous range of musical and emotional qualities, have attracted some of the best efforts of composers for nearly three centuries.

This survey does not attempt to cover that vast repertoire in anything approaching a complete way, but is intended more as a brief excursion through the repertoire of the cello, with signposts in many directions. I hope it will tempt the reader to explore the territory more fully on his own.

The versatility of the cello's role in ensembles

The cello as 'bass'
It is regrettable that cellists have often been made to feel that the role of the bass is an inferior one, an attitude which has caused them to neglect proper investigation of the musical and structural importance of the bass line and has prevented them from developing an understanding of the immense authority it imparts to any composition. Playing the bass line is something I personally find fascinating and creative. Because it is one of the most demanding roles in chamber music, requiring the utmost imagination and musicianship on the part of the player, the cellist has an opportunity through the bass line to shape the structure of the music

and the direction of the ensemble. For better or for worse, it is upon the imagination and creativity of the cellist – his musicality, his rhythmic strength, his sense of musical architecture – that the whole musical destiny of the work will either stand or fall. The bass is the spine of any piece of music, and just as the spine in the body provides a centre of strength from which the muscles move out and have their free play of movement and interaction, so the bass line in music, properly played, provides a centre of stability and source of movement which allows one's partners to enjoy a logic of free play within the scope of the musical expression.

This applies in an almost stronger yet more subtle sense when one is playing continuo in a Baroque ensemble, where an even greater sensitivity to sound, colour, texture and rhythm – and an understanding of how these qualities can be brought into play to support the upper lines – is demanded of the cellist. Continuo playing is one of the greatest arts, and yet there are few cellists who have given sufficient thought to it to be aware of its subtleties.

The wide range of the cello in ensemble playing

While the cello's primary role in ensemble playing is that of bass, composers have been quick to utilize its ability to play in the middle and treble ranges as well. This has led to, amongst other things, a vast repertoire for two, three, four and more cellos – a repertoire that began in the seventeenth century but which extends into our modern era. Twentieth-century composers such as Xenakis and Villa Lobos have recognized the potential in even larger choirs of cellos and have written beautifully for them. The idea of ensembles comprised entirely of cellos has gained much appeal in recent years, and groups which base their concerts on compositions for multiple cellos now exist in London, New York, Berlin and Los Angeles.

Within mixed ensembles the cello's capacity for moving in and out of the various voice ranges and its ability to change roles rapidly has also been a major attraction for composers. Anyone who has heard the Beethoven Triple Concerto will have in mind an excellent illustration of this use of the cello. The Messiaen *Quartet for the End of Time* is another work which highlights the cello in all its ranges, as do the cello–violin duos of Stamitz, Ravel, Martinú, Honegger, Kodály, and Mátyás Seiber. Here are two examples taken from works which are perhaps less well-known to cellists.

K. Stamitz: Duo No. 1 in C for Cello and Violin, first mov't., bars 10–13

Mátyás Seiber: Duo for Violin and Cello, second mov't., bars 185–95

The Cello

And at least one composer has understood the magical worlds of colour, texture and range that can come about from combining the cello with the clarinet:

Phyllis Tate: Sonata for Clarinet and Cello, first mov't., bars 1–4

The Solo Cello

One of the most striking attributes of the cello is the fulness with which a player can combine all the various voice ranges and roles on the single instrument. The Solo Sonata of Kodály is one of the most outstanding examples of this kind of writing for the cello. Kodály uses a single cello throughout to play bass and treble, to accompany itself, to play counterpoint against itself – in short, a full orchestration in all ranges on one instrument.

Other twentieth-century composers, such as Franz Reizenstein, Benjamin Britten, Hans-Werner Henze, Halsey Stevens, Alexander Tcherepnin and Toshiro Mayuzumi, to name but a few, have written beautiful and exciting works with a revealing fantasy and understanding for the capacities of the solo cello. One finds a similar awareness of the cello's solo potential in the Suites for Solo Cello by Max Reger. Though in a less exotic manner than Kodály, and therefore in a less orchestral vein, these suites exploit the capacities of the instrument in a most remarkable way.

272

The Cello–Piano Sonata

The cello–piano sonata is the form most commonly linked with recitals today. The use of the cello with the piano, and the vast and extremely significant repertoire for this combination of instruments, went hand-in-hand with the growth of the piano in the nineteenth century and with the piano's immense popularity throughout the nineteenth and twentieth centuries.

From Beethoven onwards there has hardly been a great composer who has not written for cello and piano as a duo. Together the two instruments have such potential for variety of colour and texture, and such contrapuntal scope, that this form seems to have drawn the finest inspiration from the greatest composers. There is a marvellous sense of completeness about cello–piano sonatas when each player brings to the ensemble a sense of true partnership.

Because this repertoire is so rich, one should be eager to explore as many sonatas by as many composers as possible. Yet I find many cellists today unaware of, and perhaps even unwilling to investigate, the many, many sonatas (and other pieces for cello and piano as well) which lie outside the so-called 'standard repertoire'. At least a dozen names jump to mind: Pizzetti, Rubbra, Stevens, Tansman, Delius, Reizenstein, Villa Lobos, Reger, Saint-Saëns, Bridge, Fauré, Kokkonen, Honegger. No need to lament our 'limited repertoire' – that is a cliché which cellists themselves have perpetuated.

The Concerto

The cliché of a 'small repertoire' carries over into the realm of the concerto as well, and here it is equally false. So great is the number of concertos for cello that it would not be possible for any one cellist to investigate them properly within the span of a single lifetime. Over 500 concertos from the eighteenth century alone are known to exist, and there are many hundreds more from the nineteenth and twentieth centuries.* Yet the deplorable fact remains that, while all these concertos go uninvestigated and unplayed, the same small handful which are *supposed* to comprise the repertoire are heard over and over again – and cellists and public alike bewail our 'limited' repertoire.

The limitation of our repertoire lies more with the attitudes of cellists themselves – and, to be fair, with those critics who so often approach unfamiliar concertos with a closed mind. It lies, as well, with concert promoters and planners who too frequently prefer to stick with the tried and true favourites.

There are, however, encouraging signs that the concert-going public is becoming ripe for greater contrast and innovation in programme-building and would welcome a greater degree of intermingling of less familiar repertoire with the well-known. Imaginative programme-planning is all that is needed. People who have this task should attempt to envisage how unknown works (from any period) can actually enhance a concert when they are properly placed between familiar masterpieces. In fact, greater variety in programming has the additional advantage of keeping a fresher face on those works which are now so over-played. Inclusion of 'new' works can actually stimulate the interest of the public, especially now that access to performances of the known repertoire is becoming increasingly greater through recordings and through the sheer number of concerts going on today.

Cellists can contribute greatly to this process by becoming more aware of the vastness of their repertoire – and by becoming more courageous in investigating the unknown. They hold it in their hands to bring the lesser-known repertoire to light; and, in the process of expanding the public's concept of 'standard repertoire', they will also find

*Many of the eighteenth-century concertos from the Pyron Collection are already available through the Philadelphia Free Library. Anyone interested in modern concertos will find that some seventy-five have already been reviewed by S. S. Dale in *The Strad*.

themselves enlarged and enriched – musically and instrumentally.

One final word: in pleading for an expansion of our concept of the cello's repertoire, I do not wish to cast even a flicker of doubt on the value and beauty of those magnificent concertos and other works which comprise the already familiar repertoire. I am only hoping that cellists, conductors, concert promoters, and the concert public will widen their vision a bit and thereby come to know the delights of a much larger and richer concerto repertoire than is dreamt of today. Those works which are unfamiliar are not necessarily poorer than the familiar ones, it is only that they have never been given a chance to be heard. (How many people, for instance, have ever heard the Shostakovich Second Concerto? How many even know it exists? Yet, were it not for the fact that it has been shunted into obscurity by the familiarity of the first concerto, I suspect that many people would find it superior.) It is up to cellists to know the scope of their own repertoire. Of course we cannot play everything, but we should know that it exists – and we should not all walk in step down the well-worn paths of a handful of familiar favourites.

Three
A Personal List of Neglected but Recommended Cello Works

This list by no means encompasses all of the neglected works for cello which are worthy of performance (or valuable as study works). It is rather a very personal list of works and composers who I feel have been unjustly overlooked by cellists. The degree of neglect of any given work will vary, of course, from one country to another (the Samuel Barber Sonata, or Bloch's *Schelomo*, are quite popular in America, but rarely heard in Europe). For reasons of practicality, I have listed only those works which are currently available in print, but once cellists begin to investigate their own repertoire they will find many more works, currently out of print, in their libraries. And they will, of course, want to add to this list works which they have discovered and come to regard on their own.

I. *Cello and Piano*

Auric, Georges: *Imaginée* (Sal)
Barber, Samuel: Sonata, Op. 6 (GS)
Badings, Henk: Sonata No. 1 (DN)
    Sonata No. 2 (Pet No. AL1)
Bartók, Béla: Rhapsody No. 1 transcribed for cello by the
    composer (BH)
Ben-Haim, Paul: *Canzona* (IMP)
    Three Songs Without Words (IMP)
Bentzon, Niels Viggo: Sonata, Op. 43 (Dansk)

Berwald, Franz: Duo (Gehrmans)

Bloch, Ernst: *Voice in the Wilderness*, composer's version for cello and piano after the symphonic poem for orchestra (GS)

Bruch, Max: *Kol Nidre* (Int) (also for cello and orchestra)

Busoni, F.: Suite for Cello and Piano, Op. 23 (BH)

Camilleri, Charles: Sonata, Op. 32 (Fairfield)

Carter, Elliot: Sonata (AMP)

Cooke, Arnold: Sonata (Nov)

Dalby, Martin: Variations (Leng)

Davidov, Karl: His four concertos currently available make excellent student works with either piano or orchestral accompaniment.

Delius, Frederick: Sonata (BH)

Dohnányi, Ernst von: Sonata in B-flat, Op. 8 (Int)

Fauré, Gabriel: Sonata No. 1, Op. 109 (Dur)
Sonata No. 2, Op. 117 (Dur)

Fortner, Wolfgang: Sonata (SCH 569)

Frankel, Benjamin: Inventions, Op. 31 (Ches)

Ginestera, Alberto: Pampeana No. 2 (Barry)

Golterman, Georg: Student Concertos 1–5 for either cello and piano or cello and orchestra.

Grieg, Edvard: Sonata in A minor, Op. 36 (Int)

Hindemith, Paul: *Drei Leichte Stücke* (SCH 2271)

Honegger, Arthur: Sonata (ESC)
Sonatina (RL)

Huré, John: Sonata in F-sharp minor (Int)

Jacob, Gordon: Sonata in D minor (JWL)

Klengel, Julius: Student Concertos and other works with piano or orchestra.

Kodály, Zoltán: Sonatina (EMB)

Kokkonen, Joonas: Sonata (fazer)

Kilpinen, Yriö: Sonata, Op. 90 (BRH)

Lalo, Edouard: Sonata (Huegel)

Martinú, Bohuslav: *Nocturnes* (Leduc)
Sonata No. 1 (Heugel)

Mendelssohn, Felix: *Variations concertantes*, Op. 17 (Pet 1735)

The Cello

Sonata in B-flat, Op. 45 (Pet 1735)
Sonata in D, Op. 58 (Aug)
Song Without Words, Op. 109 (Pet 1735)
Miaskovsky, Nikolai: Sonata No. 1, Op. 12 (MZK)
Sonata No. 2, Op. 81 (MZK)
Milhaud, Darius: Sonata (Sal)
Mozart, W. A. (son): *Grande Sonate*, Op. 19 (SCH 6001)
Nin, Joaquin: *Chants d'Espagne* (ESC)
Pizzetti, Ildebrando: Sonata in F (Ric 119404)
Tre Canti (Ric 119895)
Popper, David: *Hungarian Rhapsody* (CF 03485) (origi-
nally for cello and orchestra)
Reger, Max: Sonata in A minor, Op. 116 (Pet 3283)
Sonata in F, Op. 78 (BB)
Rawsthorne, Alan: Sonata (Oxf 21.006)
Reizenstein, Franz: *Cantilene*, Op. 18 (Leng)
Elegy, Op 7 (Leng)
Sonata in A, Op. 22 (Leng)
Romberg, Bernhard: Student concertos with either piano
or orchestra; sonatas and sonata movements.
Ropartz, J. Guy: Sonata No. 1 in G minor (Dur)
Sonata No. 2 in A minor (Dur)
Rubbra, Edmund: *Soliloquy*, Op. 57 (Leng) (originally for
cello and orchestra)
Sonata in G minor, Op. 60 (Leng)
Rubinstein, Anton: Sonata, Op. 18 (Haml)
Saint-Saëns, Camille: Sonata No. 1 in C minor, Op. 32
(Dur)
Sonata No. 2 in F, Op. 123 (Dur)
Schmitt, Florent: *Chant élégiaque*, Op. 24 (Dur) (originally
for cello and orchestra)
Seiber, Mátyás: Sarabande and Gigue in Old Style (SMP)
Tre Pezzi (SCH-L 10379) (originally for cello and
orchestra)
Shostakovitch, Dmitri: Two Pieces – 'Adagio'; 'Spring
Waltz' (Pet 4767)
Sibelius, Jean: *Malinconia*, Op. 20 (BRH)
Stevens, Halsey: Intermezzo, Cadenza and Finale (Peer)

Moravian Folksong (CFE)
Music for Christopher (Peer)
Roumanian Dance (CFE)
Sonata (Peer)
Sonatina No. 1 (Helios)
Three Pieces (Pet 6029)
Strauss, Richard: Sonata in F, Op. 6 (Int)
Tansman, Alexander: *Fantasie* (ESC)
    Sonata (ESC)
Tcherepnin, Alexander: Sonata in D (Dur)
    Sonata No. 2, Op. 30, No. 1 (UE 7349)
    Sonata No. 3, Op. 30, No. 2 (UE 9572)
    Songs and Dances, Op. 84 (Pet BEL 213)
Villa-Lobos, Heitor: Sonata No. 2 (ESC)
Webern, Anton von: Three Little Pieces, Op. 11 (UE 7577)
Wölfl, Joseph: Sonata in D minor, Op. 31 (Baer HM111)
Wordsworth, William: Nocturn, Op. 29 (Leng)
    Scherzo, Op. 42 (Leng)

II. *Unaccompanied Cello*

Badings, Henk: Sonata No. 2 (DN) (Pet. No. D6)
Banks, Don: Sequence (SCH-L 11074)
Bentzon, Niels Viggo: Sonata Op. 110 (WH)
Bloch, Ernst: Suites No. 1, 2 and 3 (Broude Brothers)
Crumb, George: Sonata (Pet 6056)
Dallapiccola, Luigi: *Ciaccona, Intermezzo e Adagio* (UE 11686)
Flothuis, Marius: Sonata Op. 2 (Broe 233)
Fortner, Wolfgang: Suite (SCH 2255)
Gabrielli, Domenico: *Ricercare* (SMP and MCA)
Gross, Robert: Epode (CFE)
Henze, Hans Werner: Serenade (SCH 4330)
Jolivet, André: *Suite en Concert* (BH)
Klengel, Julius: Caprice in the Form of a Chaconne, Op. 43 (BRH)
Kodály, Zoltán: *Capriccio* (EMB)

The Cello

Krenek, Ernst: Suite, Op. 84 (GS)
Leighton, Kenneth: Sonata, Op. 52 (Nov)
McCabe, John: Partita (Nov)
Mayuzumi, Toshiro: *Bunraku* (Pet 6356)
Nin-Culmell, Joaquín: Suite (ESC)
Reger, Max: Three Suites, Op. 131c (Int and Pet 3970)
Rubbra, Edmund: Improvisation, Op. 124 (Leng)
Reizenstein, Franz: Sonata (Ms; enquiries to Leng)
Stevens, Halsey: Sonata (Pet 6375)
Tcherepnin, Alexander: Suite (Dur)
Toch, Ernst: Impromptu, Op. 90 (Mil)
Wellez, Egon: Suite, Op. 39 (UE 8881)

III. *Cello and Orchestra*

d'Albert, Eugène: Concerto in C, Op. 20 (Pet)
Auber, Daniel-Francois-Esprit: Concerto in A (Ric R718)
Ben-Haim, Paul: Concerto (IMP)
Blacher, Boris: Concerto (BB)
Barber, Samuel: Concerto, Op. 22 (GS)
Bloch, Ernst: *Schelomo* (GS) (all cellists know of this, but so few play it!)
  Voice in the Wilderness (GS)
Boellmann, Léon: *Variations Symphoniques*, Op. 23 (CF, Dur, Kal)
Bruch, Max: *Kol Nidre*, Op. 47 (CF, Kal)
Bush, Alan: Concert Suite, Op. 37 (JWL)
Danzi, Franz: Variations on a Theme from Mozart's *Don Giovanni* (BRH)
Delius, Frederick: Concerto (BH)
Dohnányi, Ernst von: Concertpiece, Op. 12 (Int)
Dvořák, Antonin: Rondo, Op. 94 (Int)
  Silent Woods, Op. 68, No. 5 (Artia, SIM)
Honegger, Arthur: Concerto (Senart)
Ibert, Jacques: Concerto (Huegel)
Kabalevsky, Dmitri: Concerto No. 1, Op. 49 (MZK)
Khatchaturian, Aram: Concerto (MZK)
  Concerto-Rhapsody (MZK)

Korngold, Erich Wolfgang: Concerto in C, Op. 37 (SCH 4117)

Larsson, Lars-Erik: *Concertino* (Gehrmans)

Lindner, August: Concerto in E, Op. 34 (Delrieu) (this is a good student work – only the first movement is published)

Malipiero, G. F.: Concerto (SZ)
  Fantasie concertanti – III (Ric)

Martin, Frank: Concerto (UE)

Miaskovsky, Nikolai: Concerto, Op. 66 (MZK)

Monn, Georg Matthias: Concerto in G (GS and UE)

Murrill, Herbert: Concerto No. 2 (Oxf)

Pfitzner, Hans: Concerto in G, Op. 42 (SCH 2420)

Prokofiev, Sergei: *Concertino*, Op. 132 (MZK)
  Sinfonia Concertante, Op. 125 (BH & MZK)

Raff, Joseph Joachim: Concerto, Op. 193 (CF)

Reizenstein, Franz: Concerto, Op. 8 (Leng)

Rosenberg, Hilding: Concerto No. 2 (Gehrmans)

Roussel, Albert: Concerto, Op. 57 (Dur)

Rubbra, Edmund: Soliloquy, Op. 57 (Leng)

Shostakovitch, Dmitri: Concerto No. 2, Op. 126 (MZK)

Stamitz, Karl: Concerto No. 1 in G (Baer HM104)
  Concerto No. 2 in A (Baer HM79)
  Concerto No. 3 in C (Baer HM105)

Stevens, Bernard: Concerto, Op. 18 (Leng)

Stevens, Halsey: Concerto (CFE)

Tcherepnin, Alexander: *Rhapsodie géorgienne* (Dur)

Volkmann, Robert: Serenade in D, Op. 69, No. 3 (CF)

Walton, William: Concerto (Oxf)

Wiren, Dag: Concerto, Op. 10 (Gehrens)

(Though it is not possible to mention all of them here, I would like to call cellists' attention to the many really excellent Scandinavian composers who have been by-passed by cellists as a whole. There is more talent there, and more good music for the cello, than most cellists dream of.)

Index

The Cello